A Beginner's Guide to
JAPANESE
HAIKU

思無邪

Confucius said, "As for poetry, no twisted thoughts."

"No twisted thoughts," 思無邪 is often found on scrolls
hanging in tea rooms and martial arts dojos, to keep
the minds of the participants from wandering to other
things. It means "not harboring anything negative in
one's mind," and is a major tenet of the Way of Haiku.

A BEGINNER'S GUIDE TO
JAPANESE HAIKU

Major Works by Japan's Best-Loved Poets

William Scott Wilson
Foreword by Steven Heine

TUTTLE Publishing

Tokyo | Rutland, Vermont | Singapore

Dedicated to Joanne Qualmann Brown

To Access Audio Recordings for the Poems:

1. Check to be sure you have an Internet connection.
2. Type the URL below into your web browser.

www.tuttlepublishing.com/a-beginners-guide-to-japanese-haiku

For support, you can email us at info@tuttlepublishing.com.

CONTENTS

LESS WELL-KNOWN HAIKU POETS

THE BRUSH AND THE SWORD

IT IS OFTEN SAID THAT THE KEY ASPECTS of traditional Japanese culture are the brush and the sword, or the literary, philosophical and attentive side of human existence, which appreciates and celebrates the richness of nature as a mirror or model for personal awareness, and the martial, disciplined or anticipatory side of experience that summons individual strength through restraint and commitment to a communal ideal. However, a saying that proclaims, "the brush and sword are one," indicates not only that many martial artists have also been among the expert practitioners of the literary or fine arts, but also that the two experiential sides are inseparable. The discipline of swordsmanship can and is often necessary to guide the brush, just as the freedom of drawing strokes for poetry or painting greatly enhances cultivation of the virtues of dedication and restraint. As twentieth-century tea master and Zen philosopher Shin'ichi Hisamatsu once said, "The way of tea is unthinkable without conformity to the rules," yet sometimes genuine creativity for either brush or sword comes only when one knows how and when it is appropriate to be liberated from such constraints.

In his outstanding career as one of our leading and most skillful translators of Japanese writings from various eras and different types of authors, William Scott Wilson has very capably encompassed, with his large array of book publications, both sides of Japanese culture and more, including the topics of history, travel, theater, religious thought and mythology. His works, endlessly enticing and inspiring, are designed to be read by a wide range of bibliophiles, including those with a strong understanding of

Japanese society and others who are curious to explore this field for the first time.

My initial knowledge of Wilson's expertise came well over three decades ago when I found in a bookstore *The Unfettered Mind: Writings from a Zen Master to a Zen Swordsman*, the most famous treatise of Takuan Soho from the seventeenth century. I regularly used this as a required text in classes I was teaching at Penn State University. At the end of the 1990s, I moved to Florida International University in Miami, where Wilson lives as a mainstay of the local Japanese cultural community, and I had the pleasure of starting a long friendship with him. Over the years, we have had numerous wonderful conversations about Japanese literature, and I always find that he is enthusiastic about a couple of book projects in the pipeline. When traveling to Japan, I continued to see his books sold at Narita Airport and other venues.

In the current volume, following on the heels of his successful translation, *The Life and Zen Haiku Poetry of Santoka Taneda*, on an eccentric and eclectic modern writer, Wilson offers a stunning overview of over two dozen haiku poets. This begins with Basho, the originator of the literary technique, and covers more recent exemplary figures. Wilson translates and provides insightful biographies of poets who are conventional in abiding by the 5-7-5 syllable structure or innovative in modifying this format.

I recommend that readers examine the writers one at a time, but also weave back and forth between sections to uncover many fascinating connections. One example is the role of Masaoka Shiki, the haiku teacher of Natsume Soseki who is better known as Japan's leading twentieth-century novelist. Shiki tried his best to preserve the legacy of Basho's approach to writing haiku by emphasizing the role of *shasei*, or "describing a living situation not unlike a photograph." Another connection is seen in multiple verses about frogs (*kawazu*), crickets (*mushi*), mountains (*yama*) or the moon (*tsuki*) or roads (*michi*) or temple bells (*kane*) during any of the four seasons.

I am reminded of one of my favorite Basho verses that is not included in this volume:

> A cloud of cherry blossoms;
> The chime of a temple bell,
> Is it Asakusa or is it Ueno?

花の雲 鐘は上野か浅草か

Hana no kumo kane wa Ueno ka Asakusa ka

This haiku was written when Basho lived in Fukagawa, a neighborhood in old Edo (modern-day Tokyo) to the southeast and across the Sumida River from two famous areas that marked Edo's Low City (*shitamachi*) district during the shogun era, each with its own massive Buddhist temple compound: Kaneiji temple in Ueno, established by the shogunate to ward off evil spirits that might enter the city's northeastern corridor; and Sensoji temple in Asakusa, which became the unofficial center of the thriving culture of play, encompassing entertainment from Kabuki theater to licensed prostitution. Both temples featured a large bronze bell that was rung by striking a wood clapper to signal important times of the day, such as sunrise, noon and sunset. This served as the main timekeeper for people in the vicinity who did not have clocks. The resonance of the bell would echo for miles.

We can imagine that one day Basho and his companions have gone for a stroll and the falling blossoms of profuse cherry trees (*hana* means flowers generally, but for springtime poems it indicates cherry blossom) are floating in the breeze, thus forming an ethereal atmosphere for their promenade. (Today, the magnificent Kiyosumi Garden is in this area of Tokyo, with a stone monument to Basho and his most famous haiku about a frog leaping in an old pond to create the sound of water. There is also the Basho Memorial Museum nearby, in addition to a small Shinto shrine dedicated to his writings.)

Perhaps a gust of wind has come along to scatter the petals when a disciple begins the discussion by saying, "Isn't it blissful, Master Basho, to walk in the midst of so many cherry blossoms?" Then a single flower falls and Basho considers, "Even the most frail bloom holds a deep truth." Suddenly, the chiming of a bell is heard from across the water that separates Basho's neighborhood of Fukagawa from the main part of Edo. Is this not the sound of one of the two well-known temples, Asakusa or Ueno?

As Wilson instructs, "There is no meaning . . . It is the poetry of the moment and that moment's experience."

—Steven Heine
Author of *Dogen: Japan's Original Zen Teacher*

AN INTRODUCTION TO HAIKU

THE CLASSICAL JAPANESE HAIKU is a short poem consisting of three stanzas of five syllables, seven syllables, five syllables. It will generally include a *kigo*, or "season word"—for example, a flower that blooms in spring, or a gale that is specific to fall—to provide a temporal setting; and often a *kireji* or "exclamation word" such as *kana*, *ya* or *keri*. Also, generally, the poems will have no "meaning," but will simply invoke a moment that is of significance to the poet.

Haiku first began to be written as an independent literary form in the mid-fifteenth century, and its popularity among both readers and amateur poets has continued on to this day. Despite the well-known saying, understandable for a largely rural society,

Rather than working on verses, work the fields

the practice of writing haiku has extended from professional poets to all classes in Japan. It has also found popularity throughout the non-Japanese-speaking world where study groups and classes in the subject are not uncommon. In the United States alone, it is likely that more people are familiar with haiku than they might be with Elizabethan sonnets. For such a seemingly humble genre of literature, how has this come to be?

Language and Form

One pleasant day in late spring or early summer around the year AD 457, the young emperor Yuryaku was enjoying himself in the fields outside of the capital, when he encountered a young lady gathering flowers and herbs. The emperor was so taken by her charming countenance that he composed a poem which, in the language of the day, amounted to a marriage proposal.

> With your basket, carrying your lovely basket;
> with your spade, carrying your lovely spade;
> young thing, gathering herbs on this hillside,
> tell me where you live, tell me your name.
> In this land of Yamato, broad as the sky,
> I am the one who rules all and one;
> I am the one who reigns far and wide.
> Thus I will tell you
> my home and my name.

This was selected to be the opening poem in the *Man'yoshu*, the very first imperial collection of Japanese poems. This classic, compiled about AD 759, includes some 4,516 poems, ranging in subjects from love, the sadness of parting, celebrations, and the grief of death; authored by emperors, aristocrats and even farmers. Considered to reflect the true spirit of the Japanese, it was written in what is called *man'yogana*, a script entirely of Chinese characters, the only one available at the time.[1] To make matters more complicated, some of the characters were read for meaning, but most others for phonetic value. The opening of Yuryaku's poem, for example, appears like this:

籠毛與、美籠母乳、布久思毛與、美夫君志持

and is pronounced:

---

1. Chinese characters were introduced to the Japanese, who had no written language of their own, by a Korean scholar, Wani, in the early fourth century.

Komoyo, mikomochi, fukushimoyo, mibukushimochi

Thus, in the original, it was and is a work that can only be read by the ultra-educated.

It is also interesting that the poem does not have the usual cadence and rhythm of classical Japanese poetry, which, like all other poems in the *Man'yoshu*, is composed of lines of five and seven syllables. Other than this first poem, the *Man'yoshu* consists of either *choka*, long poems of multiple lines, and over four thousand *waka*, short poems of five lines with thirty-one syllables following a pattern of 5-7-5-7 7.

By the ninth century, poetry—that is to say, *waka*—had become a way of life for the aristocracy, and the cumbersome man'yogana a hindrance in its writing, recitation and study. Coming to the rescue was the introduction of the hiragana syllabary, reputedly invented by the Buddhist priest, Kukai (Kobo Daishi), who traveled to China for study in 804, but possibly having been naturally developed over the previous hundred years or so. Hiragana characters are so-called syllabets (neither true syllables nor an alphabet) representing sounds only, developed from radically simplified cursive forms of Chinese characters. The sound a (あ) for example, is the simplified form of the Chinese character 安, the sound *na* (な) from the character 奈, the sound *mu* (む) from the character 武, and so on, for all of the forty-eight syllables in the Japanese language. This development greatly facilitated writing, reading and recitation, and allowed for a written system of visual balance and beauty, using a combination of both Chinese characters and hiragana, an artistic compliment to the poem in which it was written. The first poem in the *Kokinshu*, a collection of over a thousand waka published in 905 reads:

Spring has come,
> before this year's end.
So this one year,
> should it be called last year,
> should it be called this year?

年の内に、春はきにけり、ひととせを、
去年とやいはむ、今年とやいはん
Toshi no uchi ni, haru wa kinikeri, hitotose wo,
kozo to ya iwan, kotoshi to ya iwan

This would continue to be the written form of Japanese poetry, and engendered a burst of poetic creativity and appreciation for the next thousand years. It is, generally, the written form of the Japanese language today.[2]

❦   ❦   ❦

At around the end of the Heian period (794–1185), composing *renga*, or linked verse, became a popular form of amusement for aristocrats and the upper classes. Two or more poets would create verses based on the waka form, but the first poet would offer the *hokku*, or beginning verse, of 5-7-5 syllables and the next poet would continue with a verse of 7-7. The following poet would then add a verse of 5-7-5, another would add one of 7-7, and so on. The theme or mood of each verse had to be continued by the next, no matter how vaguely.

The facing page starts with an example of this poetry style, composed with the participation of six poets:

---

2. A number of Japanese poets, many of whom were Buddhist priests, practiced writing poetry called *kanshi* in pure Chinese, but this was limited to scholars.

The moon on the dry beach
  where geese return
full of peace.
  The boat beckons them away
  with trailing white waves.
Today, leaving the capital,
  how many days
has it been?
  More and more the storm
  on my sleeves of the journey.
On faraway fields
  the sun burns the haze
at the beginning of dusk.
  But with what color,
  the cloud-darkened pines?

Often these would extend to a hundred verses long, and some-times even to a thousand.

The first imperial renga anthology was compiled in 1356 and the style was fully developed during the fifteenth century. By this time, *rengakai*, the gatherings of haiku poets, were not limited to the aristocracy, but had spread to all levels of society, and it was from this point that hokku, also called *haiku*, began to be written and recorded on its own.

Renga continued (and still continues) to be practiced in Japan—it was composed and taught by one of the "great four" haiku poets, Matsuo Basho—and in foreign languages too. In 1971, the book, *Renga: A Chain of Poems*, was published by Mexican poet Octovio Paz, comprised of twenty-seven poems written in Spanish, English, French and Italian, by different poets. The poems were actually sonnets, but the idea of collaborative works was taken from the Japanese model.

Language and Intent

When the Korean scholar Wani introduced Chinese characters to the Japanese in the early fourth century, he brought with him a number of documents, including the *Analects of Confucius*, the very last words of which are:

If you do not know words, how will you know mankind?

This made a lasting impression on the already very poetic Japanese. "How will you know mankind?" was taken to mean, "How will you communicate with others?" and this communication eventually meant "poetry." In the preface to the *Kokinshu*, the editor, Ki no Tsurayuki, writes:

The Japanese poem made the human heart its seed, and developed into words as many as the myriad leaves. Many are the deeds and impressions of those who live in this world, and what is heartfelt, seen, and heard by them, they put into words. Hearing the song of the flower-hidden nightingale or the voice of the water frog, who that is living would not express himself in poetry? Poetry is that which, without the slightest effort, moves heaven and earth, stirs the unseen gods and spirits to feelings of pity,[3] brings accord to husband and wife, and calms the mind of the fierce warrior.

---

3. "Stirs the unseen gods and spirits to feelings of pity" was not an exaggeration on Tsurayuki's part. Ritual Shinto prayers or chants to secure good crops and social harmony called *norito* had been in usage for ages past. It was and is felt that the words themselves have a sort of magical power to move the gods and to spur them on to fulfill the request of the petitioner, who recites the prayers almost in a trance. The meaning of the words and grammar are sometimes unclear, no doubt due to their origin in the distant past.

Poetry, then, became a sort of lingua franca, especially among, but not confined to the nobility, communicating every emotion or desire, at times accompanied by the hope that even the karma of the words would affect the hearer's heart and actions. For hundreds of years after the *Kokinshu*, many other imperial collections of poetry were commissioned and compiled, evidence of the popularity of this medium.

But despite the popularity of poetry, there were those who worried that its quality was on the decline. In the same preface quoted on the facing page, Tsurayuki writes:

> In this generation, "beauty" is foremost, and people's hearts have become imbued with the florid, their poetry frivolous and insubstantial at best. Thus, Japanese poetry has become interred in the homes of the sensuous, something little considered; no longer is it displayed by the more serious-minded. With its origins in mind, we cannot think this is proper.

This disappointing state of affairs would be remedied in an unexpected way.

Nearly 250 years after Tsurayuki had written his piece on words and some 900 years after Wani had brought Confucius' dictum on the same, two Buddhist monks returned from study in China, bringing with them a new austere sect called Zen, or Ch'an in Chinese. One of the foremost statements of this new sect was,

不立文字

No depending on words or letters.

This concept would be expanded to imply that not only the fewer words the better in true communication, but less of any physical material in any art would bring the mind into closer contact with the true spiritual or psychological intent of that art. This would become a basic tenet of much of classical Japanese culture, as can be seen in the extreme economy of movement and dialogue in Noh drama, the sparse use of ink in the art of sumi-e painting, or the artistic placement of a few large rocks in an enclosure of white sand in so-called "dry gardening."

Another fundamental concept of Zen Buddhism was expressed in the phrase,

直指人心

Direct pointing to the mind of man.

This also meant getting away from wordiness and "over-think" in general, relying more on intuition and practice than dogma and reasoning, and a general emphasis on, again, simplicity and frankness.

Thus it is natural that these two Zen concepts would help lead the art of poetry from the flowery and sometimes ethereal waka and renga to the very spare art of haiku. And it is not surprising that Iio Sogi (1421–1502) and Matsuo Basho (1644–1694), the two men who detached the hokku, the first 5-7-5 stanza of renga, and developed it into an independent haiku were both students of Zen.

The Poets

Unlike the majority of waka poets, the men and women who followed "the way of haiku" were not aristocrats or high-ranked members of the warrior class who had vied to have their verses included in the *Kokinshu* and other imperial poetry collections.

Among the poets included in this book, each of whom has their work prefaced by a short biography, you will find professional poets, members of the samurai class, farmer's children, sons of Confucian scholars, periodical writers, merchants' children, Buddhist wanderers, novelists, insurance salesmen, housewives and alcoholic tramps to name a few. Many were perpetual travelers, and all lovers of nature. But social rank held no cache. The authenticity of the writer's verse was and is the gauge.

Poetry of the Moment

Haiku is the poetry of simplicity and frankness, an almost wordless verse—the sound of the unstrung zither, in the parlance of Zen—that resolves the seeming paradox of Confucius' necessity of the knowledge of words, and Zen Buddhism's non-reliance on words and letters. Haiku encapsulates the mundane and the ordinary, finding in them significance rather than meaning. There is no meaning in Basho's sound of water, Soseki's buttocks on his bike, Buson's straw sandal at the bottom of a frozen pond or Santoka's relieving his bowels under falling leaves. It is the poetry of the moment and that moment's experience. To quote the Japanese philosopher, Nishida Kitaro,

> A truly pure experience has no meaning whatsoever. It is simply a present consciousness of facts just as they are.[4]

This pure experience is the essence of haiku. There is (very rarely) any judgment of the experience because if there were, the poem would become one of meaning rather than significance.

The haiku poets—like Buddhist and Shinto practitioners—

---

4. Nishida, *An Inquiry into the Good*, page 4.

valued practice over theory or dogma[5] as it was a mindful practice of the art, rather than speculating about it, that would bring one closer to the very core of life.

To return to the question of why the study and practice of this genre, developed nearly five hundred years ago, remains so popular (look up *haiku* on any online bookstore and you will find dozens of entries), three reasons may be suggested. For the Japanese, haiku's deep association with nature must be very attractive to a people whose many art forms—painting, gardening and flower arranging to name a few—are tied to the natural world and whose pastimes include cherry-blossom viewing and the admiration of autumn foliage. Added to this to this might be their long history of valuing a poetical outlook as a way of being in and perceiving the world. For both the Japanese and for Westerners, the attraction would include haiku's extreme accessibility: its very short form and its emphasis on artlessness and encapsulating the mundane, thus providing a venue for expressing instantaneous moments of significance without having to struggle with longer and more complicated forms. Last but not least, the study of haiku affords the student an opportunity to look into the insights and personalities of some of the most popular and eccentric writers in Japanese literary history, and perhaps, again, to give expression to their own.

The Translations

For translating all of the haiku included in this anthology, I have adhered to the traditional three-line format. Even in the shorter and longer poems of Santoka and Seisensui, it seems that the

---

5. There were and are various schools of haiku, emphasizing the value of moods, the inclusion or exclusion of season words or the required number of syllables in a verse. But all theories take a back seat to the daily practice of honing the mind to see or feel what is directly before it, as implied in the Zen quote 看脚下, "look beneath your feet."

natural in and out rhythm has been retained in the original, and that translating them in a single line, or in four or five lines, would make them appear as something they are not: clever epigrams or abbreviated waka. In addition, I have not attempted to use the syllable count of 5-7-5 in the English versions of the poems, as this would be tedious and ill advised at best. The genius of one country's language does not readily fit well into that of another.[6]

The original Japanese has been included here for two reasons: First, to give the reader a hint of the aesthetic beauty of the form in which the poems would have been written down; and—as no translation can be considered final—to provide readers of Japanese the opportunity of perhaps coming up with their own translations. Even with such short poems, the paucity of grammar and the choice of vocabulary can lead to multiple interpretations. Second, the romanized versions of the poems will present even the non-Japanese speaker with an idea of how the poem sounds in the original,[7] and thus how it would have been recited at the haiku gatherings so loved of the poets themselves.

—William Scott Wilson

---

6. Gregorian chants are often broken down into 5-5-5 syllables, but this is perhaps the exception that proves the rule.
7. Vowels are pronounced the same as in Spanish; *f* like an *h* but with pursed lips; and *r* somewhere between an *l* and a *d*—the tip of the tongue will lightly touch the roof of the mouth near the upper teeth. There are other slight differences, but these are minimal.

Acknowledgments

I owe a deep debt of gratitude to Kate Barnes, Jim Brems, Bill Durham, Elizabeth Frankl, Robin Gill, Gary Haskins, Takashi Ichikawa, Barry Lancet, Thomas Levidiotis, Daniel Medvedov, Laura Nenzi, Justin Newman, John Siscoe, my late professors Nobuo Hiraga and Richard McKinnon, Jack Whisler and many others for their support, instruction and unending encouragement over the years. And a special bow of thanks to Cathy Layne at Tuttle Publishing for her dogged, dedicated and judicious editing of this anthology.

THE "GREAT FOUR" HAIKU POETS

MATSUO BASHO (1644–1694)

YOSA BUSON (1716–1783)

KOBAYASHI ISSA (1763–1827)

MASAOKA SHIKI (1867–1902)

MATSUO BASHO
(1644–1694)

MATSUO BASHO was born in Iga Ueno, Mie Prefecture, and spent his youth there. Ueno, a castle town in the Iga Basin, encompassed on four sides by mountains, was the center of the Iga-ryu style of ninjitsu—ninja techniques taught as a martial art. His father, Matsuo Yozaemon, was a country samurai of lower status, said to be descended from the ancient Heike clan. Basho was Yozaemon's second son and, along with his older brother, he had one older sister and one younger sister. When Basho was thirteen, his father died, leaving his older brother as the caretaker of the family, which was now not in affluent circumstances.

Traditional accounts of Basho's life say that after his father's death he served as a page to the young son of one of the generals of the fief. Another theory has it that he was also employed as an underling in the kitchen. The general's son, Todo Yoshitada, was two years older than Basho, had a taste for elegant accomplishments and took on the pseudonym of a haiku poet, Sengin, or "Cry of the Cicada." It is possible that Basho was made Yoshitada's companion in haiku, and that his talent for figures of speech and poetry received special attention. But Yoshitada died at the age of twenty-five in the spring of 1666. Accordingly, Basho lost hope for any further favorable treatment because of his association with this general's son and resigned his position. According to later biographers, he left his home town, traveled to Kyoto and studied Chinese and Japanese literature under various poets and scholars. As he was a simple lordless samurai from the country, however, this is doubtful, and his true history at this time is unclear.

Nevertheless, in 1672, he traveled to Edo (modern-day

Tokyo), making it his pied-à-terre, but seems to have spent some of his time wandering. He may also have spent some time studying at the Chokeiji Zen temple under the tutelage of the priest Butcho in the Fukagawa section of Edo. At this temple, Chinese classics such as the philosophy of Lao Tzu and Chuang Tzu and the poetry of Li Po, Tu Fu and Han Shan were taught, thus expanding Basho's sense of natural philosophy, the rhythm of poetry and the spirit of journeys. To make a living, he is said to have periodically worked in the construction of waterworks at Sekiguchi in Edo between 1677 and 1680.

It was during this period that interest in haiku was rising and new styles were being emphasized, and the thirty-year-old Basho must have sympathized with this movement. Edo was a new, exciting capital city where many traditions were being thrown to the wind, old styles were being abandoned and the new advocated. There were already a number of well-known poets in Edo, and the eager and enthusiastic Basho happily joined their ranks.

In the winter of 1680, Basho, now thirty-six years old, entered a hermitage in Fukagawa, thanks to the support of one of his admirers. Given a banana tree (*basho*) by his disciple Rika, he planted it at the hermitage, which became known as the Banana Hermitage (Basho-an), and it was at this time that the poet took the name Basho. Until now he had written under his given name, Munefusa, or the nom de plume Tosei. At the Banana Hermitage Basho could live the poetic life of *wabi*, or simplicity and quiet, and could express his rejection of worldly desire and status in the so-called "floating world"—the transient world of everyday affairs. It was an environment of his own choosing, and one in which he felt his sense of true haiku could grow.

> A night of listening;
>   the banana leaves in the autumn wind
>   rain falling into the tub.

In December of 1682, however, the Basho-an burned to the ground during the great Edo fire of that year. This was said to be a turning point in Basho's life, bringing home the Buddhist concept he had studied of the transience of all things. This transience, or *mujo* 無常, and the consequent concept of a mind essence free from any thought of attachment, *muju no shintai* 無住の心体, would become an integral undercurrent in his verse from this point on.

Basho's disciple Kikaku later wrote that this disaster made it clear to Basho that he was essentially homeless in the world. Basho later wrote on his bamboo hat as he journeyed with a friend,

乾坤無住同行二人
Through the universe, two travelers with no dwelling.

In May of the following year, Basho turned his back on the disaster and traveled to the far north of Japan. Returning to Fukagawa in the winter, he was able to take up residence in a new hermitage. In June, he had returned to his home town on receiving news of his mother's death, an event which would also have underscored his understanding of transience. On this trip he wrote,

> Fukagawa!
> We're off, leaving the banana plant
> to Mount Fuji.

The hermitage in Fukagawa continued to be Basho's headquarters, but he also continued making journeys at regular intervals, often with disciples or companions, and between March and December of 1689, he once again traveled to the far north of Japan, a trip that resulted in his most famous travel diary, *The Narrow Road to the Deep North*. After this journey, Basho lived quietly, spending some time in Kyoto, where he traveled to teach some of his disciples, and returning to his home town in Iga; but in the fall of 1691, he returned to Edo to a new Basho-an and planted another banana tree.

For the next two-and-a-half years, Basho stayed at his hermitage and took care of two invalids also living there—a nephew Toin, and a woman called Jutei, who was reportedly an old sweetheart from his Kyoto days. Toin passed away in 1693, and Basho remained in Edo to nurse his other charge.

In May of 1694, Jutei's health seemed to make an improvement, and Basho departed on another journey to Iga. Within a month, however, Jutei, too, passed away. After conducting a service for her during the August Bon festival to honor the dead, Basho continued on what would be his last journey, which by all accounts was filled with hardships, including difficult relationships within the haiku community and with his relatives, his weakening constitution, as well as the death of his intimate friends.

Yet he carried on, writing and visiting friends in Nara and Osaka. In the latter city, however, Basho developed dysentery, and died at the age of fifty on October 12, 1694. Previously, he had written,

> Falling ill on a journey,
>   my dreams wander out
>   over a withered moor.

The moon and the sun are travelers of a hundred ages, and the years, too, that come and go are wayfarers. Those who spent their lives floating on a boat or who met old age leading a horse, made every day a journey, and the journey their home.

—*The Narrow Road to the Deep North*

It is important to note that Basho spent much of his life on journeys, and that most of his best haiku are included in the travel diaries that he wrote. From the time he was twenty-three to the age of fifty he was frequently on the road, observing the ever-changing aspects of nature and the passing of the seasons. During these journeys and with his own life experiences, he developed a sense of the essential mutability of life, which was reflected in his later haiku and in the poetic prose, or *haibun*, in which these journals were written. He seems to have felt that when life is understood as being fundamentally transient, each moment, each being—sentient or insentient—possesses its very own significance which should be met with immediacy and compassion. This leaves no room for contrivance or intentional beautification of words and phrases, and as Basho walked along on his pilgrimages, although he must have felt the grandeur of nature, his response was a simple human sympathy. Two verses that clearly illustrate this response:

> The bush warbler
> in the bamboo shoot thicket,
> sings of old age.

> Spring rain,
> it trickles down the wasps' nest
> through the leaking roof.

In the end, Basho would have agreed with another great traveler, R. L. Stevenson, who famously said, "Travel light." This phrase is not so much about what you carry on your back as what you carry—or don't carry—in your head.

> First autumn rains;
> Let my name be called,
> "Traveler."

❧   ❧   ❧

Haiku by Basho

An autumn night
spent talking
with others.

秋の夜を打崩したる咄かな
Aki no yo wo uchikuzushitaru hanashi kana

On this road
no one goes;
autumn's end.

この道を行人なしに秋の暮
Kono michi wo yuku hito nashi ni aki no kure

Deep autumn;
my neighbor,
how is he managing?

秋深かし隣はなにをする人ぞ
Aki fukashi tonari wa nani wo suru hito zo

Conditions on the Kiso?[1]
clouds and sprouting
grasses of spring.

木曽の情雲や生ぬく春の草
Kiso no jo kumo ya haenuku haru no kusa

Though it's cold,
nights sleeping together
warm the heart.

寒けれど二人寝る夜ぞ頼もしき
Samukeredo futari neru yo zo tanomoshiki

---

1. The Kiso is the sixty-mile heart of the Nakasendo, the ancient road between Edo and Kyoto. It is also the name of the river that runs through it.

Well then, let's go:
    snow viewing until
    we all fall down.

いざ行かむ雪見にころぶ所迄
Iza yukan yukimi ni korobu tokoro made

I know not
    what flowering tree this is;
    but its fragrance!

何の木の花とはしらず匂哉
Nan no ki no hana to wa shirazu nioi kana

Soaring above
    the skylark,
    the mountain peak.

雲雀より空にやすらふ峰かな
Hibari yori sora ni yasurau mine kana

Tired out from a journey;
    just as finding an inn,
    flowers of wisteria.

草臥て宿かる比や藤の花
Kutabirete yado karu koro ya fuji no hana

Though summer has come,
    only one leaf,
    just one leaf!

夏来てもただひとつ葉の一葉哉
Natsu kite mo tada hitotsu ha no hitoha kana

Unaware of the drinking party,
the morning glories
in full bloom.

朝顔は酒盛しらぬさかりかな
Asagao wa sakamori shiranu sakari kana

The suspension bridge!
One's life depending
on creepers and vines.

桟やいのちをからむつたかづら
Kakehashi ya inochi wo karamu tsutakazura

Still thin
from traveling the Kiso;
but later on, the moon.

木曽の痩せもまだなをらぬに後の月
Kiso no yase mo mada naoranu ni nochi no tsuki

On a journey, even the hardened person
must take lessons
from flies on the Kiso.

うき人の旅にも習へ木曽の蠅
Uki hito no tabi ni mo narae kiso no hae

Horse chestnuts of the Kiso:
souvenirs for the people
of the mundane world.

木曽のとち浮世の人のみやげ哉
Kiso no tochi ukiyo no hito no miyage kana

Sending off and being sent off;
the end of autumn
in the Kiso.

おくられつおくりつはては木曽の秋
Okuraretsu okuritsu hate wa kiso no aki

The moon!
Now a sign saying come this way;
an inn on a journey.

月ぞしるべこなたへ入せ旅の宿
Tsuki zo shirube konata e irase tabi no yado

Blown about by the spring breeze,
the flowers, too,
laugh.

春風にふき出し笑ふ花も哉
Harukaze ni fukidashi warau hana mo kana

It goes along
and goes along, until…
the year's end.

成りにけりなりにけり迄年の暮
Nari ni keri nari ni keri made toshi no kure

Autumn has come;
searching out your ear,
the wind at your pillow.

秋来にけり耳をたづねて枕の風
Aki kinikeri mimi wo tazunete makura no kaze

A crow
    perched on a withered branch;
autumn's end.

枯枝に烏のとまりたるや秋の暮
Kare-eda ni karasu no tomaritaru ya aki no kure

Drunk among the flowers,
    wearing a half coat and sword;
a woman.

花に酔り羽織着てかたな指す女
Hana ni yoeri haori kite katana sasu onna

Flowers in the mundane world;
    my saké, unrefined;
    my rice, sooty.

花にうき世我酒白く飯黒し
Hana ni ukiyo waga sake shiroku meshi kuroshi

I am a man
    who eats his meal
    among morning glories!

あさがほに我は飯くふおとこ哉
Asagao ni ware wa meshi kuu otoko kana

The horse ambles along,
    I look like a painting;
    the summer plain.

馬ぼくぼく我をゑに見る夏野哉
Uma boku boku ware wo e ni miru natsuno kana

The scent of an orchid;
      something like the wing
of a butterfly.

蘭の香やてふの翅にたき物す
Ran no ka ya cho no tsubasa nitakimono su

To the flowers in full bloom
    in the world;
      reciting the nenbutsu.[2]

世にさかる花にも念仏申けり
Yo ni sakaru hana ni mo nenbutsu moshikeri

Asleep on a bed of grass;
     is a dog soaked with winter rains, too?
Sounds at night.

草枕犬も時雨るかよるのこゑ
Kusamakura inu mo shigururu ka yoru no koe

The sea darkens;
     the quacking of ducks,
    faintly white.

海くれて鴨のこゑほのかに白し
Umi kurete kamo no koe honoka ni shiroshi

---

2. The nenbutsu is a short chant or mantra, repeating the name of the Amida
   Buddha as a sort of meditation or prayer of gratitude.

The year comes to an end;
while wearing a rain hat
and straw sandals.

年暮ぬ笠着て草鞋はきながら
Toshi kurenu kasa kite waraji hakinagara

The flower of the plum
perfumes the world; on one branch,
a sparrow.

世ににほへ梅花一枝のみそさざい
Yo ni nioe umehana isshi no misosazai

Back from a journey,
the crow finds his old nest
turned into a flowering plum.

旅がらす古巣はむめに成にけり
Tabigarasu furusu wa mume ni narinikeri

Spring has come!
On a nameless mountain,
thin mist.

春なれや名もなき山の薄霞
Haru nare ya na mo naki yama no usugasumi

Overnight at an inn;
hear my verse,
the autumn wind!

たびねして我句をしれや秋の風
Tabine shite waga ku wo shire ya aki no kaze

An old pond;
    a frog jumps in:
  the sound of water.

古池や蛙飛びこむ水のをと
Furuike ya kawazu tobikomu mizu no oto

"Is he a blind masseuse?"
    Seen by others,
    gazing at the moon.

座頭かと人に見られて月見哉
Zato ka to hito ni mirarete tsukimi kana

The seagulls
    unable to sleep;
  the cold water.

水寒く寝入かねたるかもめかな
Mizu samuku neiri kanetaru kamome kana

Drinking saké,
    yet unable to sleep;
  a night of snow.

酒のめばいとど寝られね夜の雪
Sake nomeba ichido nerarene yoru no yuki

The stillness!
    The cries of cicadas
  sink into the rocks.

閑さや岩にしみ入る蝉の声
Shizukasa ya iwa ni shimiiru semi no koe

Under the same roof,
　　a prostitute is sleeping, too,
　moonlight on bush clover.

一家に遊女もねたり萩の月
Hitotsuya ni yujo mo netari hagi no tsuki

Drinking morning tea,
　　how peaceful the monk;
　frost on chrysanthemums.

朝茶のむ僧しづかさよ菊の霜
Asacha nomu so shizukasa yo kiku no shimo

How admirable the man
　　who does not become enlightened
　at the flash of lightning.

稲妻にさとらぬ人の貴さよ
Inazuma ni satoranu hito no tattosa yo

Having strayed from their nests
　　in the dark of night;
　crying plovers.

闇の夜や巣をまどはしてなく衒
Yami no yo ya su wo madowashite naku chidori

Falling ill on a journey,
　　my dreams wander out
　over a withered moor.

旅に病んで夢は枯野をかけ廻る
Tabi ni yande yume wa kareno wo kekemeguru

YOSA BUSON
(1716–1783)

By MOST ACCOUNTS, Yosa Buson, originally named Taniguchi Buson, was born in the village of Kemamura in Settsu Province, now in Hyogo Prefecture. In this rural farming district his family was relatively wealthy, and as a young child he could roam through woods, fields, and along rivers, observing nature and dabbling in painting. Buson later wrote:

> When I was young, on days that were clear with the colors of spring I would inevitably go out with friends and play in the vicinity of the banks of the rivers.[1]

According to different sources, he left home at either seventeen or twenty, and went on a wandering journey to Edo (now Tokyo), where he studied art and poetry—both Chinese and Japanese—under several masters. By the time he was twenty-three, in 1738, examples of his paintings and haiku began to appear in art circles.

In 1742, however, his main teacher passed away, and Buson left for Shimosa, just north of Edo, where he continued his studies, traveling around the vicinity, painting and composing haiku. It is conjectured that another reason he left Edo was the popularization and subsequent vulgarization of haiku in the poetry circles there. Whatever his motivations, he now engaged in a ten-year wandering journey, often in harsh and miserable circumstances, but always deeply attentive to his natural environment.

---

1. From *Buson to haiga* [Buson and haiga] by Suzuki Susumu. Tokyo: Shogakkan, 1976.

By 1751, at age thirty-six, Buson quit his life of wandering and moved to the old capital of Kyoto, where he found the artistic community to be far more focused on poetry than on the Chinese philosophies of Confucianism or Taoism.

It was in Kyoto, perhaps, that Buson resolved to lead his life as a member of the literati, or *bunjin*. The term in Sino-Japanese is written 文人, indicating a person of letters, but the bunjin were interested in all the arts, from poetry to painting to swordsmanship and so on. The character 文, now understood as "letters" or "literature," anciently indicated "patterns"—anything from the pattern of a flock of birds in flight to that of the ripples made from a stone thrown into a pond—and by extension, beauty. How better to express the patterns and beauty of nature, mankind and their intertwining, than poetry and painting? The ideal circumstances for the bunjin at this time in Kyoto were intoxication with haiku (and wine), and so Buson found the city congenial to his own aspirations. Yet it was not all artistic partying in Kyoto. He noted,

> However, as it was my own personal habit of disliking to be in contact with the vulgar, I kept myself apart from mixing with the people of the world, would close my gate, and stay in my own rooms [. . .] and found it more appropriate to pass time with my own inclinations.[2]

Expressing this in a haiku he composed during this time, he wrote

> For the most part,
> when alone,
> the moon is my companion.

---

2. From *Buson to haiga* [Buson and haiga] by Suzuki Susumu. Tokyo: Shogakkan, 1976.

After living in Kyoto for three years, Buson moved to the province of Tango, an area of beautiful natural scenery, facing the Sea of Japan. This was where his mother was said to be born, in the town of Yosa, and it was here that he changed his family name from Taniguchi to Yosa. Tango, and specifically the city of Miyazu, where Buson chose to live, was a place often visited by bunjin, and perhaps due to both the environment and visits from like-minded artists, he felt that his techniques both in haiku and painting improved. It was here, too, that his paintings began to take on more lightness of character and an unconstrained free-and-easy expression, and could rightfully be called *haiga*—paintings imbued with the spirit of haiku.

In 1757, Buson left Tango and returned to Kyoto. About this time, as his reputation as a painter had increased, he made much of his living painting folding screens, and he was economically stable enough to get married and have a child, a daughter.

> How delightful;
> the child's white face
> under the tiny mosquito net.

But nine years later, aged fifty-one, his wanderlust returned and he spent three years wandering the island of Shikoku, painting, attending haiku gatherings and absorbing Chinese literature and art. Around this time his style of painting became known as the "Yosa style" and his haiku style a "return to Basho." It is indicative of Buson's devotion to Basho that from 1778 to 1779, he dedicated himself to illustrating Basho's most famous journal, *The Narrow Road to the Deep North*, on scrolls and folding screens.

After his sojourn in Shikoku, Buson returned to Kyoto where he was feted as a master of both haiku and haiga. Finally, in 1783, he became ill, and passed away on December 25 at the age of sixty-eight.

❧   ❧   ❧

It is said that Buson is a poet whose work captures the world of phenomena.

> How refreshing!
>   The sound of the bell
> leaving the bell.

Basho's poetry, on the other hand, goes to the very heart of things. R. H. Blyth, in his *Haiku (Volume 1)*, gives perhaps the best examples of the contrast between their styles:

> The old pond;
>   a frog jumps in—
> the sound of water.
>   Basho

> An old pond;
>   a sunken straw sandal—
> sleet.
>   Buson

Basho's verse gives us the moment, an arresting significance that would be impossible to convey visually or in ordinary prose. Buson gives us a photograph (or a painting in his case)—a scene that might have been produced with ink and paper. Both men were great poets, and one often feels the adult Zen practitioner in Basho, but sees the child playing in the fields and water's edge in Buson: two aspects of a fully human being living in the world.

❧   ❧   ❧

Haiku by Buson

The barrier guard's brazier
so small;
the lingering cold.

関守の火鉢小さき余寒哉
Sekimori no hibachi chiisaki yokan kana

The long day of spring;
echoes heard in the corners
of the capital.

遅キ日や谺聞ゆる京の隅
Osoki hi ya kodama kikoyuru miyako no sumi

The monk taking a nap
on an evening of spring;
his white elbows.

肘白き僧のかり寝や宵の春
Hiji shiroki so no karine ya yoi no haru

Waking from a cold nap,
the spring day
almost gone.

うたた寝のさむれば春の日くれたり
Utatane no samureba haru no hi kuretari

Lighting one candle
with another;
a night of spring.

燭の火を燭にうつすや春の夕
Shoku no hi wo shoku ni utsusu ya haru no yuu

The tub for washing my feet
is leaking, too;
passing spring!

洗足の盥も漏りてゆく春や
Sensoku no tarai mo morite yuku haru ya

Passing spring;
women in the same carriage,
whispering.

行春や同車の君のさざめ言
Yuku haru ya dousha no kimi no sazamegoto

Spring rain;
feeling sorry for myself,
and can't write a thing.

春雨やもの書けぬ身のあわれなる
Harusame ya mono kakenu mi no aware naru

The spring sea;
gently, quietly,
all day long.

春の海終日のたりのたり哉
Haru no umi hinemosu notari notari kana

"The day is coming to a close!"
      "The night is dawning!"
   croak the frogs.

日は日くれよ夜は夜明ヶよと啼く蛙
Hi wa hikure yo yo wa yoake yo to naku kawazu

When it swims,
      it looks helpless;
   the frog.

およぐ時よるべなきさまの蛙かな
Oyogu toki yorube naki sama no kawazu kana

The sick man
      fanning away flies;
   the heat!

病人のかたの蠅追ふ暑さかな
Byonin no kata no hae ou atsusa kana

Even the duckweed
      has sunk to the bottom;
   May rains.

うきくさも沈むばかりよ五月雨
Ukikusa mo shizumu bakari yo satsuki ame

The shortcut;
      walking through the stream
   in May rains.

ちか道や水ふみ渡る皐雨
Chikamichi ya mizu fumiwataru satsuki ame

A sudden shower;
    grasping at the leaves of weeds,
  a flock of sparrows.

夕だちや草葉をつかむむらすずめ
Yuudachi ya kusaba wo tsukamu mura suzume

How pleasant!
    Crossing summer rivers,
  straw sandals in hand.

夏河を越すうれしさよ手に草履
Natsukawa wo kosu ureshisa yo te ni zori

An old well,
     fish jumping at mosquitoes;
a dark sound.

古井戸や蚊に飛ぶ魚の音くらし
Furuido ya ka ni tobu uo no oto kurashi

Cicadas crying,
     the Buddhist ascetic passes by,
at noon.

蝉鳴や行者の過る午の刻
Semi naku ya gyoja no suguru uma no koku

Autumn has come;
     showing their agreement,
sneezes!

秋来ぬと合点させたる嚔かな
Aki kinu to gaten sasetaru kusame kana

How pitiful!
     Stepping on my dead wife's comb,
in the bedroom.

身にしむや亡妻の櫛を閨に踏
Mi ni shimu ya nakitsuma no kushi wo neya ni fumu

Lonely even more
     than last year;
passing autumn.

去年より又さびしひぞ秋の暮
Kyonen yori mata sabishii zo aki no kure

Leaving the gate,
I, too, am a wayfarer;
passing autumn.

門を出れば我も行人秋のくれ
Kado wo dereba ware mo yukuhito aki no kure

Feeling sorry for myself,
I forgot my cane;
passing autumn.

淋し身に杖わすれたり秋の暮
Sabishi mi ni tsue wasuretari aki no kure

Made to pull up my futon
by the snowy storm;
midnight in autumn.

嵐雪にふとん着せたり夜半の秋
Ransetsu ni futon kisetari yohan no aki

Mountains birds on the branch
shifting one foot to another;
the long night.

山鳥の枝踏かゆる夜長哉
Yamadori no eda fumikayuru yonaga kana

At the mountain peak teahouse
where no one lives,
a full moon.

名月や夜は人住ぬ峰の茶屋
Meigetsu ya yo wa hito sumanu mine no chaya

Is this the branch road
        crossing the wide plain
in deep mist?

霧ふかき廣野にかかる岐かな
Kiri fukaki hirono ni kakaru chimata kana

A bottomless pail
        tumbling along;
the late autumn blast.

底のない桶こけ歩行野分かな
Soko no nai oke kokearuku nowaki kana

The wife and child, too,
        eating something at the temple;
the late autumn blast.

妻も子も寺でもの食ふ野分かな
Tsuma mo ko mo tera de mono kuu nowaki kana

The lightning
        spilling the sound;
dew on the bamboo.

稲妻にこぼるる音や竹の露
Inazuma ni koboruru oto ya take no tsuyu

Walking the Kiso Road;
        well then, I'm fine with getting old;
alone in the fall.

木曽路行ていざとしよらん秋ひとり
Kisoji yukite iza toshiyoran aki hitori

My life in the fall;
I'll put up with tonight,
there's always tomorrow.

身の秋や今宵をしのぶ翌もあり
Mi no aki ya koyoi wo shinobu asu mo ari

My neighbors dislike me;
a whistling pot
on a cold night.

我を厭ふ隣家寒夜に鍋を鳴らす
Ware wo itou rinka kanya nabe wo narasu

Not even water birds can be seen,
the cold
crossing the bay.

水鳥も見えぬ江わたる寒さ哉
Mizutori mo mienu e wataru samusa kana

A cold moon;
feeling the small pebbles
at the soles of my boots.

寒月や小石のさはる沓の底
Kangetsu ya koishi no sawaru kutsu no soko

The old umbrella blown about;
a moonlit night
and a wintry shower.

古傘の婆娑と月夜の時雨哉
Furugasa no basa to tsukiyo no shigure kana

A night winter shower;
  irritated at the sound
of the toads.

夕時雨蟇ひそみ音に愁ふ哉
Yuu shigure gama hisomine ni ureu kana

Branches broken from the snow
  heard far away;
night deepens.

雪折も遠く聞こへて夜ぞふけぬ
Yuki ore mo touku kikoete yo zo fukenu

In the old pond,
  straw sandals sunk to the bottom;
sleet.

古池に草履沈ミてみぞれ哉
Furuike ni zori shizumite mizore kana

A wintry blast;
  stepping across the stones
of a river in the plain.

こがらしや野河の石をふみわたる
Kogarashi ya nogawa no ishi wo fumiwataru

Even my bones are cold,
  touching the futon;
a night of frost.

我骨のふとんにさはる霜夜哉
Waga hone no futon ni sawaru shimoyo kana

The reverend priest
squatting to shit;
the withered moor.

大とこの糞ひりおはすかれの哉
Daitoko no kuso hiriowasu kareno kana

Having crossed the mountain,
we go our separate ways;
the withered moor.

山をこす人にわかれて枯野かな
Yama wo kosu hito ni wakarete kareno kana

Winter confinement,
I feel detached
from the Buddha.

冬ごもり佛にうときこころ哉
Fuyugomori hotoke ni utoki kokoro kana

With socks still on, I sleep
a melancholy night,
seeing dreams.

足袋はいて寝る夜ものうき夢見哉
Tabi haite neru yo monouki yumemi kana

When I die, too,
at my tombstone place
withered pampas grass.

我も死して碑に辺せむ枯尾花
Ware mo shi shite hi ni hotori sen kareobana

KOBAYASHI ISSA

(1763 – 1827)

KOBAYASHI ISSA WAS BORN the eldest son of Kobayashi Yagohei, a well-to-do farmer in the village of Kashiwabara in the province of Shinano. His mother died when he was three years old, and his father remarried five years later. The relationship between Issa and his stepmother was never a good one, and with the birth of a her child when Issa was ten, the feelings between the two became even more tense and unloving. His grandmother did her best to intervene, but she passed away not long after the birth of the stepbrother, leaving Issa to wander the fields alone, taking solace in nature. It may have been at this time in his life when he began to feel sympathy for the smaller animals he found around him, a sympathy he would express throughout his life.

> Little fleas,
> the night must be long for you, too,
> and lonely.

Finally, to bring harmony to his home life, Yagohei sent the fourteen-year-old Issa to Edo (modern-day Tokyo) to earn a living, and it was there that he began to study haiku. Fourteen years later, he returned to his native village for the first time, but his relationship with his stepmother was all the more unpleasant, and he left again after a short time, traveling to Kyoto. This began a four-year period of wandering—first around Kyoto and the Kansai region—then a return to Edo, and finally back to Kyoto for another three years of traveling.

In 1802, his father fell ill, and Issa returned once again to his childhood village, staying with his father until the latter's death. Unsurprisingly, his stepmother refused to divide the inheritance equally between Yagohei's two sons, and Issa left for Edo, continuing to wander for another few years. While wandering, he had been composing haiku and, although he had no disciples, had become well known in haiku circles.

When Issa was fifty-one, a mediator finally settled the dispute over the inheritance left by Yagohei, and he was able to settle down in his native place and marry. This union produced four sons and one daughter, but tragically, all died young. After the second daughter died, Issa wrote,

> I know it is a world of dew,
> a world of dew, yet...
> yet...

And then his wife died only three years later.

> Left alive,
> left alive;
> the cold!

Issa was now sixty-one years old. He remarried the following year, but the marriage was not a happy one and the couple was soon divorced. The very next year, Issa married for the third time. For two years, Issa lived a contented life, but in 1827, his house burned down in a fire that had swept through the village, and he and his wife had to live in a storehouse that had escaped the conflagration. In November of the same year, Issa was struck with paralysis, and did not survive. His wife gave birth to a daughter after he had passed away.

❧   ❧   ❧

Issa's love of nature and its smaller creatures was reflected in his poetry and it is often noted that among his numerous haiku, fifty-four were on snails, fifteen on toads, two hundred on frogs, two hundred and thirty on fireflies, more than one hundred on fleas, ninety on cicadas and about seventy on other creatures. He was extremely prolific, writing over twenty thousand haiku, compared to Basho's two thousand.

Although Issa admired Basho, his haiku were markedly different from those of the master. Basho's verse is said to go straight to the heart of life, while Issa's travels along its surface. The perfect contrast may once again be found with Basho's famous haiku on the frog and the pond:

> The old pond,
> a frog jumps in;
> the sound of water.

This is a moment in time, the significance of which can only be indicated by words, but not explained. However, we find nothing about how Basho felt about the frog, the living creature inhabiting the poem. Compare this to Issa's

> Scrawny frog,
> don't be defeated;
> Issa is here.

This verse and many others demonstrate Issa's love of nature's beings and his compassion for all things. We see Issa's heart here, while in the poem on the jumping frog, we see Basho's mind. Basho, the son of a samurai, was a student of Zen Buddhism, with its austere and self-reliant vision, emphasizing mental concentration and looking inward rather than at the outside world. Issa, on the other hand, living on a farm in his early life, became a lay priest in the Jodo Shinshu sect, which teaches the compassion of the Buddha and the inclusion of all beings in paradise. And while Basho, to my knowledge, does not mention Zen in his haiku, Issa is happy to express his religious outlook in very clear terms.

> The dew falls in drops,
>   like tears, the dove
> chants the *nenbutsu*.[1]

> It's so long, the night
>   is so long;
> *Namu Amida.*

Issa experienced periods of poverty and suffering in his life, but seemed to find his salvation and happiness in the lives of other sentient beings.

> My dwelling place:
>   the mice and fireflies
> get along just fine.

❧   ❧   ❧

Haiku by Issa

> Even on New Year's,
>   it stands just as it is;
> my tumbledown house.

元日も立ちのままなる屑家哉
Ganjitsu mo tachi no mama naru kuzuya kana

---

1. The nenbutsu is a short chant or mantra, repeating the name of the Amida Buddha as a sort of meditation or prayer of gratitude.

At every gate,
　　muddy clogs;
　　spring has come.

門門の下駄の泥より春立ちぬ
Kadokado no geta no doro yori haru tachinu

Again, this year,
　　world of troubles, you're blocked out!
My grass hut.

又ことし娑婆塞げぞよ草の家
Mata kotoshi shaba fusage zo yo kusa no ie

Today, too, today, too,
　　living in mist;
　　my little home.

けふもけふもかすんで暮らす小家哉
Kyo mo kyo mo kasunde kurasu ko-ie kana

A spring day!
　　New straw sandals
　　for the outhouse.

春の日や雪隠草履の新しき
Haru no hi ya setchin zori no atarashiki

If you'll excuse me,
　　I'm going to poop;
The little sparrow.

慈悲すれば糞をする也雀の子
Jihi wo sureba fun wo suru nari suzume no ko

57

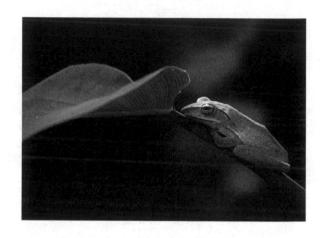

This year,
    it's a wonderful world;
        little frogs, big frogs.

ことしや世がよいぞ小蛙大蛙
Kotoshi ya yo ga yoi zo kokawazu ookawazu

The butterfly flies;
    my body, too,
        just like dust.

蝶とんで我身も塵のたぐひ哉
Cho tonde waga mi mo chiri no tagui kana

My morning:
    blooming cherry blossoms
  and weeds.

我朝は草もさくらを咲きにけり
Wagacho wa kusa mo sakura wo sakinikeri

The sky, wonderfully
    growing dark;
  the heat!

大空の見事に暮るる暑さ哉
Oozora no migoto ni kururu atsusa kana

The mountains of the Shinano Road
    becoming baggage;
  the heat!

しなの路の山が荷になる暑さ哉
Shinanoji no yama ga ni ni naru atsusa kana

The cool breeze;
    with all its strength,
  the grasshopper.

涼風や力一ぱいきりぎりす
Suzukaze ya chikara ippai kirigirisu

A cool breeze,
    meandering there,
  coming back here.

涼風の曲りくねつて来たりけり
Suzukaze no magarikunette kitari keri

The poorest of the poorest
of poor countries;
but the cool!

下下も下下下下の下国の涼しさよ
Gege mo gege gege no gekoku no suzushisa yo

Sleeping arms and legs stretched out;
how cool,
how lonely.

大の字に寝て涼しさよ淋しさよ
Dai no ji ni nete suzushisa yo sabishisa yo

Getting out of the bath,
stuck to my buttocks,
irises.[2]

湯上りの尻にぺつたり菖蒲哉
Yu agari no shiri ni pettari shoubu kana

The respected priest takes his time
shitting in an open field;
behind the parasol.

僧正が野糞遊ばす日傘哉
Sojo ga noguso asobasu higasa kana

---

2. In May, iris leaves were sometimes put into baths.

Even the mosquito smudge
is comforting;
being alone.

蚊いぶしもなぐさみになるひとり哉
Ka'ibushi mo nagusami ni naru hitori kana

If someone comes,
turn into a frog!
My cooling melon.

人来たら蛙となれよ冷し瓜
Hito kitara kawazu to nare yo hiyashi uri

"The mosquitoes are out, they're out!"
says the idler,
walking along, slapping them.

隙人や蚊が出た出たと触れ歩く
Himajin ya ka ga deta deta to furearuku

A matter of congratulations:
eaten by this year's
mosquitoes, too.

目出度さはことしの蚊にも喰はれけり
Medetasa wa kotoshi no ka ni mo kuwarekeri

"Please don't hit me!"
The fly wringing its hands,
wringing its feet.

やれ打つな蝿が手を摺り足をする
Yare utsu na hae ga te wo suri ashi wo suru

Autumn this morning;
    the sky seems to have come down
with a fever.

けさ秋や瘧の落ちたやうな空

Kesa aki ya okori no ochita yo na sora

A bit chilly;
    the song of the earthworms
all night long.

うそ寒や蚯蚓の歌も一夜づつ

Usosamu ya mimizu no uta mo hitoyo zutsu

Though I try not
    to rub my ribs;
how cold the night!

あばら骨なでじとすれば夜寒哉

Abarabone nadeji to sureba yokan kana

Those fellows and their clogs,
    clip clop, clip clop;
the long night.

下駄からりからり夜永のやつら哉

Geta karari karari yonaga no yatsura kana

Flowing right in
    to the Kiso mountains:
the Milky Way.

木曽山に流れ入りけり天の川

Kiso yama ni nagareirikeri amanogawa

Autumnal rain;
    a little sumo wrestler
  passes by.

秋の雨小さき角力通りけり
Aki no ame chiisaki sumo toorikeri

My sleeping mat;
    the late autumn storm blowing
  at the soles of my feet.

寝むしろや野分に吹かす足のうら
Nemushiro ya nowaki ni fukasu ashi no ura

All by my lonesome,
    I eat my meal;
    the autumn wind.

淋しさに飯をくふ也秋の風
Sabishisa ni meshi wo kuu nari aki no kaze

At age sixty,
    I pass the night
  without dancing.

六十年踊る夜もなく過しけり
Rokujunen odoru yo mo naku sugoshikeri

Waving its whiskers,
    the grasshopper
  chirps away.

きりぎりす髯をかつぎて啼きにけり
Kirigirisu hige wo katsugite nakinikeri

Sometime this morning
it fell;
a single leaf.

けさ程やこそりとおちてある一葉
Kesa hodo ya kosori to ochite aru hitoha

Yaa! Crickets, be quiet
for a while;
first winter rain.

やあしばらく蟬だまれ初時雨
Yaa shibaraku koorogi damare hatsu shigure

Beneath the high verandah
where I slept, a wintry blast,
blowing, blowing!

寝た下を凩づうんづうん哉
Neta shita wo kogarashi zuun kana

Making a racket,
miserable in the hail,
the sparrows.

わやくやと霰を佗びる雀哉
Wayakuya to arare wo wabiru suzume kana

Something that shouldn't be:
a moonlit night,
with sleet.

けしからぬ月夜となりしみぞれ哉
Keshikaranu tsukiyo to narishi mizore kana

Sleeping all in a row,
    the mountains of Shinano, too,
night snow.

寝ならぶやしなのの山も夜の雪
Nenarabu ya shinano no yama mo yoru no yuki

A snow good for sleep;
    gently falling,
        gently falling.

むまそうな雪がふうはりふはり哉
Mumasou na yuki ga fuuwari fuwari kana

The hole
    a straight line of pee;
        snow at the gate.

真直な小便穴や門の雪
Massugu na shoben ana ya kado no yuki

A withered field,
what will there be to eat?
The hermitage.

野はかれて何ぞ食ひたき庵哉
No wa karete nan zo kuitaki iori kana

Pulling out the radish,
he points the way
with the radish.

大根引大根で道を教へけり
Daikon hiki daikon de michi wo oshiekeri

Shut in for the winter;
that night I heard it:
rain in the mountain.

冬籠其夜に聞くや山の雨
Fuyugomori sono yo ni kiku ya yama no ame

A life of refined taste;
forty-nine years
of wasted walking around.

月花や四十九年のむだ歩き
Tsukihana ya shijuku nen no muda aruki

MASAOKA SHIKI
(1867–1902)

MASAOKA SHIKI WAS BORN in what is now Matsuyama, a city on the island of Shikoku. Facing the Inland Sea, Matsuyama is in a region of mild seasons, is backed by the 6,500-foot (1,982-meter) Mount Ishizuchi and accented by an attractive castle, Matsuyama-jo. Shiki's father, Tsunenao, was a low-ranking samurai of the Matsuyama fief; his mother, Yae, was the daughter of a Confucian scholar.

When Shiki was five years old, his father passed away, leaving him, his siblings and his mother in the charge of his maternal grandparents. His mother made money by taking in sewing at home. Shiki's education began almost immediately with lessons in calligraphy from an uncle and Chinese literature from his grandfather. Within two years, he was reading the Chinese Confucian classic *Mencius*, and by age eleven was writing poetry in Chinese, later having his compositions corrected by the father of his friend and lifelong colleague, the haiku poet Kawahigashi Hekigodo.

In 1885, at the age of eighteen, Shiki traveled to Tokyo and took up cheap lodgings in the bookstore area of Kanda. He took a philosophy course with the dream of becoming a philosopher, but gave up on this idea when he failed the exam and instead began a serious study of classical *waka* poetry and haiku. After two years in Tokyo, he began to develop some of the health problems that would plague him throughout his life and returned to Matsuyama for a short recuperation, but was back in Tokyo within months. There, along with his continuing study of haiku, he fell in love with baseball, about which he would write a collection of waka.

Just now
     the three bases
are loaded;
     uncontrollably,
     my heart is pounding.

The ball is hit
     high into the clouds;
and falls gain
     into a man's
     hand.

In January of 1890, Shiki embarked on his long friendship with the writer Natsume Soseki, and in April of that year began what would become a series of journeys, usually resulting in published essays. It was at this time that he began writing haiku under the name of Shiki, his given name having been Tsunenori. Within a year, however, his ill health returned, he once again traveled to Matsuyama for convalescence, but quickly came back to Tokyo where he entered Tokyo Imperial University to study literature.

The following year he began a letter exchange with Takayama Kyoshi, another aspiring haiku poet who, along with Shiki, would influence a generation of poets. In June, Shiki skipped his exams, took off on a journey through central Japan and, on his return, began writing a novel.

In 1892, at the age of twenty-five and to no one's surprise, he failed his university exams, withdrew from school entirely, traveled to the deep north writing an essay on Basho, and continued writing and publishing essays on haiku. Shiki had always seemed to have a cavalier attitude towards exams and in his essay "Saké," he wrote that instead of studying, he and a fellow student went out drinking the night before a trigonometry test:

That night I slept soundly, but on the following day's test, out of a perfect 100 points, I received 14. 14 points was unprecedented. Saké is bad, but the teacher was horrible.

At the outbreak of the Russo-Japanese War in 1895, Shiki was hired as a war correspondent and spent a month in China. He was too late to see any action, but the filthy conditions at camp worsened his health. On the return trip home, he spit up blood aboard ship, and was deboarded at Kobe and put into a hospital. By the following year, he was suffering from hip pain and could walk only with difficulty, but continued to write and publish. Finally, in 1897, he underwent two operations for lumbago, but in the meantime published a work on Buson in collaboration with Kyoshi, Hekigodo and Soseki.

Although Shiki would still go on to write some of his best work, he never fully recovered his health. Spitting blood, high fevers and an inability to get out of bed continued for the next five years. As his health deteriorated seriously, his friends—and particularly Hekigodo—visited him often and became his nurses.

Shiki passed away on 19 September, 1902, at the age of thirty-five.

> You should tell them
> I was one who ate persimmons
> and loved haiku.

Shiki was born some 120 years after Basho's death, and during that time the latter's personage and verse had almost been deified in the world of haiku. Shiki, too, greatly admired Basho and wrote a thirty-three-page essay, "Furuike no ku no ben" [A discourse on the verse "The Old Pond"] on what he felt had been the great man's contribution:

The old pond;
a frog jumps in,
the sound of water.

This is it. At this point, Basho himself felt that he had attained something like enlightenment concerning haiku. Before this, he made efforts to write directly from the everyday something imposing or rare, but after the frog verse, for the first time, he now created verses directly from the everyday and common [. . .] Basho finally was enlightened to the exquisiteness of nature, and retreated from the base and made-up. He found that "being without thought-fullness and discrimination was nothing other than nature itself."[1]

But Shiki also felt that poets after Basho tended more towards the insipid and sentimental rather than nature itself. Thus Shiki advocated what he perceived as Buson's clarity and objectivity and the concept of "portraying life" (*shasei*), as can be seen in the four haiku selected below. Throwing out the baggage of intellect, one might see directly into the heart of things and truly depict the moment.

In my hand
the firefly;
a cold light.

The refreshing cool;
climbing up the pine tree,
a crab in the rain.

---

1. This quote and the quote on page 69 from Masaoka Shiki *Masaoka Shiki*.

Shutting the gate,
      going out and listening;
   frogs!

Left alive
      half-hearted;
   the heat!

Shiki strongly influenced poets even from his sickbed in Matsuyama, far away from the cultural centers of Kyoto and Tokyo, and his critiques on haiku are still the sources of admiration and contention.

❦   ❦   ❦

Haiku by Shiki

The owl's dreams
      while napping;
   the summer grove.

梟の昼寝の夢や夏木立
Fukurou no hirune no yume ya natsu kodachi

A full moon!
      At the bottom of the valley,
   voices.

名月や谷の底なる話し声
Meigetsu ya tani no soko naru hanashigoe

Removing the straw hat from the wall,
out come
autumn mosquitoes.

壁の笠とれば秋の蚊あらはるる
Kabe no kasa toreba aki no ka arawaruru

Having been scolded,
I crawled in
under the covers.

叱られてもぐりこんだる蒲団かな
Shikararete mogurikondaru futon kana

A night of snow,
the rustling sound
of bamboo.

さらさらと竹に音あり夜の雪
Sarasara to take ni oto ari yoru no yuki

The single train rail
so long,
the winter grove.

汽車道の一すじ長し冬木立
Kisha michi no hitosuji nagashi fuyu kodachi

How pathetic:
snow blowing against
the horse's rump.

馬の尻雪吹きつけてあはれなり
Uma no shiri yuki fukitsukete aware nari

A runny nose
mixed with tears;
lingering spring cold.

水洟の泪にまじる余寒かな
Mizubana no namida ni majiru yokan kana

Autumn cicadas;
a bit lonely
when their crying stops.

鳴くあとのやや淋しさや秋の蝉
Naku ato no yaya samishisa ya aki no semi

Just ten steps
out through the gate,
the broad autumn sea.

門を出て十歩に秋の海広し
Mon wo dete jippo ni aki no umi hiroshi

Leaking through the wall,
the smell of the cow;
early summer rain.

壁をもる牛の匂ひや五月雨
Kabe wo moru ushi no nioi ya samidare

The sparrows walk
with wet feet
down the corridor.

ぬれ足で雀のあるく廊下かな
Nure'ashi de suzume no aruku rouka kana

Solving the riddle
and showing everyone;
winter seclusion.

なぞなぞを解て見せけり冬籠
Nazonazo wo toite misekeri fuyugomori

Gathering maple leaves,
the woman feeling cold
in the evening sun.

紅葉折りて夕日寒がる女かな
Momiji orite yuuhi samugaru onna kana

The traveler
eating a tangerine as he goes,
the barren moor.

旅人の蜜柑くひ行く枯野かな
Tabibito no mikan kuiyuku kareno kana

Opening the back door,
    calling in the ducks;
autumnal showers.

背戸あけて家鴨よびこむ時雨かな
Sedo akete ahiru yobikomu shigure kana

Passing by,
    he disappears completely
into the mist.

行く人の霞になつてしまひけり
Yuku hito no kasumi ni natte shimaikeri

Arranging some bellflowers;
    my study
for a while.

桔梗活けてしばらく仮の書斎かな
Kikyo ikite shibaraku kari no shosai kana

Listening keenly
    in bed,
infinite sounds.

床によく聞けば千千の響き哉
Toko ni yoku kikeba chiji no hibiki kana

In my delight,
    I told everyone
my first dream of the year.

うれしさにはつ夢いふてしまいけり
Ureshisa ni hatsu yume iute shimaikeri

Putting down the heavy baggage
of the world,
an afternoon nap.

世の中の重荷おろして昼寝かな
Yo no naka no omoni oroshite hirune kana

The first snow!
The window: opening, closing,
opening, closing.

初雪や窓あけてしめあけてしめ
Hatsu yuki ya mado akete shime akete shime

How refreshing!
Crawling up the pine,
a crab in the rain.

涼しさや松這ひ上がる雨の蟹
Suzushisa ya matsu haiagaru ame no kani

My life
saved at the bones;
losing weight in summer.

夏痩せの骨にとどまる命かな
Natsuyase no hone ni todomaru inochi kana

When the merchants' voices
have died down;
an afternoon of cicadas.

いろいろの売り声絶えて蝉の昼
Iroiro no urigoe taete semi no hiru

The bird chirps
and drops
the red berry.

鳥啼いて赤き木の実をこぼしけり
Tori naite akaki ko no mi wo koboshikeri

The train passes,
the smoke swirls
among young leaves.

汽車過ぎて煙うづまく若葉かな
Kisha sugite kemuri uzumaku wakaba kana

Tendrils
of the morning glory
find autumn.

朝顔のつるさき秋にとどきけり
Asagao no tsurusaki aki ni todokikeri

Eating a persimmon,
a bell rings:
the Horyuji.

柿くへば鐘が鳴るなり法隆寺
Kaki kueba kane ga narunari Houryuuji

My thoughts,
this year, too,
come to an end.

思ふこと今年も暮れてしまひけり
Omou koto kotoshi mo kurete shimaikeri

The wintry wind
blowing the man's voice
out to sea.

凩や海へ吹かるる人の声
Kogarashi ya umi e fukaruru hito no koe

A summer storm;
white paper on the desk
flying away.

夏嵐机上の白紙飛び尽くす
Natsu arashi kijo no hakushi tobitsukusu

Closing the temple gate
with a creak;
departing autumn.

山門をぎいと鎖すや秋の暮
Sanmon wo gii to tozasu ya aki no kure

Flowing clouds
like sand;
a morning of autumn.

砂の如き雲流れ行く朝の秋
Suna no gotoki kumo nagareyuku asa no aki

Poking out my head,
an autumnal wind is blowing
on the tip of my nose.

首出せば秋風吹くや鼻のさき
Kubi daseba akikaze fuku ya hana no saki

Humanity's trash
    blowing in the wind
of autumn.

人間の屑に吹きけり秋の風
Ningen no kuzu ni fukikeri aki no kaze

First day of the year!
    Unsatisfied about things
since dawn.

元日や朝からものの不平なる
Ganjitsu ya asa kara mono no fuhei naru

Poking my head
    out of the futon,
a New Year beginning.

蒲団から首だせば年の明けている
Futon kara kubi daseba toshi no akete iru

Swatting flies, burning mosquitoes,
    the sins of the sick
go deep.

蠅を打ち蚊を焼き病む身罪深し
Hae wo uchi ka wo yaki yamu mi tsumi fukashi

Three thousand haiku
    reviewed; persimmons,
two.

三千の俳句を閲し柿二つ
Sanzen no haiku wo kemishi kaki futatsu

Reading an advertisement
for flea powder
in bed.

蚤とり粉の広告を読む床の中
Nomitori ko no koukoku wo yomu toko no naka

Arranging plum flowers,
I refuse a well-wisher.
I'm sick!

梅いけて礼者ことわる病かな
Ume ikete reisha kotowaru yamai kana

Tsukutsukuboushi![2]
Everywhere,
tsukutsukuboushi!

ツクツクボウシツクツクボウシバカリナリ
Tsukutsukuboushi tsukutsukuboushi bakari nari

Autumn mosquitoes
staggering in,
stabbing us all.

秋の蚊のよろよろと来て人を刺す
Aki no ka no yoroyoro to kite hito wo sasu

---

2. The sound of a species of cicada.

OTHER WELL-KNOWN HAIKU POETS

IIO SOGI (1421–1502)

UEJIMA ONITSURA (1661–1738)

MIURA CHORA (1729–1780)

TAIGU RYOKAN (1758–1831)

INOUE SEIGETSU (1822–1887)

NATSUME SOSEKI (1867–1916)

KAWAHIGASHI HEKIGODO (1873–1937)

TAKAHAMA KYOSHI (1874–1959)

TANEDA SANTOKA (1882–1940)

OGIWARA SEISENSUI (1884–1976)

OZAKI HOSAI (1885–1926)

SUGITA HISAJO (1890–1946)

IIO SOGI
(1421–1502)

SOGI BECAME extraordinarily famous in the literary circles of his times, but his early background is obscure. It is said that he was born in either Omi or Kii province, and that his family name was either Iio or Iba. His father and mother were of humble origins, but his uncle Sozei, a famous poet and teacher of *renga* linked verse, was a retainer to the Yamana clan in Tajima. Little is known of Sogi's childhood, but at a young age he went to Kyoto and studied at the Sokokuji, a Rinzai Zen temple. In his thirties, Sogi became absorbed in renga and *waka* poetry, at first studying under his uncle Sozei and later under other famous poets. By the age of forty, he had abandoned his life in a Zen temple, established hermitages on the outskirts of Kyoto, but continued to wear his religious robes and to think of himself as a Buddhist monk for the rest of his life.

Most of Sogi's career reads like a travelogue. As his fame grew as a talented poet of renga and haiku (or *hokku* as it was called in those days), he was invited by literary groups, military clans and nobility in all parts of Japan to guide them in their own poetic efforts. In his later life, he became known as the Traveling Poet. He also lectured throughout his life on the eleventh-century classic novel *The Tale of Genji* as well as on the *Kokinshu*, an early compilation of classical Japanese poetry that was written in the year 905.

By 1500, Sogi had decided to retire from his lecture circuit, but the great Kyoto fire in July of that year burned down the hermitage where he was living, the Shugyoku-an, and he took one more journey to the province of Echigo, present-day Niigata

Prefecture. There he taught, lectured and wrote his own verses for nearly two years.

In July of 1502, at the age of eighty-two, Sogi began a return journey to Kyoto, but on the way was afflicted by abdominal pains, said to be caused by parasitic worms. Medicine seemed to have no effect, but after two days of rest he was determined to carry on and arrived at the town of Yumoto in the province of Suruga. Saying that he felt a little better, he ate some mild food, spoke with his disciples and went to sleep. But at midnight he woke with terrible pains, mumbled something to the effect of,

> Sunk in thought of the passing moon,
> wandering away,[1]

and died. His remains were carried over the Hakone mountains to what is now the city of Shizuoka and interred in the Jorinji Zen temple. In summing up his life, one of his disciples quoted the Zen priest Jichi Osho:

> In the world of travel,
>   sleeping again on the road,
> on a bed of grass
>   is a dream
>   seen within a dream.[1]

Sogi was extraordinarily prolific and left over ninety works—anthologies, diaries, poetic criticisms and essays on classical literature. Although his main genre was renga, he wrote thousands of hokku. Along with his penchant for travel, his main contribution

---

1. Okada Isao. *Sogi*. Tokyo: Yoshikawa Hirobumi kan, 1998.

to haiku was the insistence on the necessity of a season word—a sine qua non that would last for nearly four hundred years. His haiku were elegant and nature based—he at one time took the poetry name of Shizensai (自然斎, [an artist] of nature)—and there is little wonder why Basho noted him, along with the painter Sesshu, the poet Saigyo and the tea ceremony master Sen no Rikyu, as one of his artistic guides. Basho was likely thinking of Sogi when he wrote in the opening lines of his famous work *The Narrow Road to the Deep North*:

> There were men who floated their lives away on boats, or who met old age leading a horse by the mouth, who made daily life a journey, and a journey their home. Many of these men of old died on the road.

Sogi practiced calligraphy, the tea ceremony and painting, and writer R. H. Blyth in his *History of Haiku Volume 1* notes that he "was almost too poetical and artistic to be human." One of his simple verses:

> The rain of last night
>   has been hidden this morning
> by fallen leaves.

Haiku by Sogi

Not waiting for the mist,
spring has come
to the capital.

霞をもまたで春たつ都かな
Kasumi wo mo matade haru tatsu miyako kana

Even with the storm,
spring has come;
the scent of plums.

嵐にも春たつ梅のにほひかな
Arashi ni mo haru tatsu ume no nioi kana

The sound of the river,
mist over the branches
deep in the mountains.

河音は梢にかすむ深山哉
Kawa'oto wa kozue ni kasumu miyama kana

Plums in the snow;
no trace of the fruit,
but their scent!

雪に梅やみはあやなき匂哉
Yuki ni ume yami wa ayanaki nioi kana

Mountains full of flowers;
the heart has
no limit.

はなにいるやまは心のはてもなし
Hana ni iru yama wa kokoro no hate mo nashi

You may think
this an unthinking world; then
a cuckoo.

思ふをばおもはぬ世かは郭公
Omou wo ba omowanu yo ka wa kakkodori

I saw so many fireflies,
but this morning,
not a trace.

多にみしほたる影なき朝日哉
Ou ni mishi hotaru kage naki asahi kana

The moon this morning,
cool in the waves
of the western sea.

月や今朝浪に涼しき西の海
Tsuki ya kesa nami ni suzushiki nishi no umi

Morning!
The moon does not resent
the short night.

みじか夜をうらみぬ月の朝哉
Mijika yo wo uraminu tsuki no asa kana

86

The clouds and rivers
    colored by the coming fall;
  faraway mountains.

雲水を色に秋たつみ山哉
Unsui wo iro ni aki tatsu miyama kana

The coolness!
    Already the trees of faraway mountains;
  the colors of autumn.

すずしさやはやみ山木の秋の色
Suzushisa ya haya miyama ki no aki no iro

The reeds a shelter
    for the wind;
      the path at daybreak.

おぎをやどの風も朝たつ山ぢ哉
Ogi wo yado no kaze mo asa tatsu yamaji kana

Paulownia leaves
    moving the rain;
  clouds in autumn.

桐のはに雨をうごかせ秋の雲
Kiri no ha ni ame wo ugokase aki no kumo

Mist, too,
    late rains all day;
  the autumnal blast.

霧も今朝しぐるばかりの野分哉
Kiri mo kesa shiguru bakari no nowaki kana

Pine crickets, too,
     accompanying the wind;
  the rustling of reeds.

松虫も風に友なへおぎのこゑ
Matsumushi mo kaze ni tomonae ogi no koe

In the autumn sea,
     the boat one leaf
  in the unseen world.

秋の海舟はみぬ世の一葉哉
Aki no umi fune wa minu yo no hitoba kana

The dew and already
     the early winter rains;
  the mountain path.

露もはや時雨ばかりの山ぢ哉
Tsuyu mo haya shigure bakari no yamaji kana

Rain striking the moss:
    the voice of autumn
in distant mountains.

苔をうつ雨や深山の秋の声
Koke wo utsu ame ya miyama no aki no koe

The moon, too,
    traveling through early winter rains
at dawn.

朝ぼらけ時雨にめぐる月も哉
Asaborake shigure ni meguru tsuki mo kana

The winter rains, too,
    are crossing the mountain;
a path through the clouds.

山こゆる時雨もたびの雲ぢ哉
Yama koyuru shigure mo tabi no kumoji kana

Last night's rain,
    hidden this morning
by tree leaves.

夜の雨を今朝ふりかくす木葉哉
Yo no ame wo kesa furikakusu ko no ha kana

A world of snow,
    bamboo leaves blown against
my door at dawn.

雪の夜の竹の葉とづる朝戸哉
Yuki no yo no take no ha tozuru asa to kana

UEJIMA ONITSURA
(1661–1738)

UEJIMA ONITSURA, whose childhood name was Takematsu, was born in the castle town of Itami, near Osaka. His father, Soshun, ran a brewery, and the area is still renowned for its saké. Onitsura started writing haiku at the age of eight; the best-known example of his work is,

> Though I called, "Come! Come!"
> the fireflies
> flew away.

By the age of twenty-six, his verses had already been included in a number of collections. That year he left for employment in Edo (modern-day Tokyo), but soon returned to the Osaka area.

In 1691, Onitsura was employed by a Fujiwara Tadahira in Yamato Province. His status is unclear, but he was apparently allowed to carry a weapon, as the following year, trying to dissuade a disturbance, he was attacked by a retainer and cut the man down with a long sword. Illustrations of Onitsura often depict him with a sword crooked in his arm. By 1694, he had returned to Osaka, and by 1695, he was back in Itami, where his first son was born. Sadly, the child died at the age of six, and the poet wrote,

> Buried in the ground,
> will this child bloom
> a flower?

Moving back and forth between various employments, Onitsura

eventually moved to Osaka with his wife and two younger sons, only to have his house burn down in 1724, after which he relocated for the last time to his home town, Itami.

In 1733, at the age of seventy-three, Onitsura took the tonsure and retired from public activity. His wife died the following year, and he himself passed away on August 2, 1738, at the age of seventy-eight. His funeral was held at the Horinji temple in Osaka and he was buried at the Bokusenji temple in Itami, both Zen Buddhist temples of the Soto sect.

"Basho in the east, Onitsura in the west," is a well-known phrase in haiku communities in Japan. Basho was sixteen years old when Onitsura was born, wrote his famous "The old pond/a frog jumps in/the sound of water" verse when Onitsura was twenty-six, and began his famous journey to the far north when the latter was twenty-nine. Onitsura deeply respected the elder poet's verses, but came into his own at an early age, publishing his own haiku collections throughout his life.

While Basho's byword for the foundation of his haiku might have been "nature," Onitsura declared, at age twenty-five, that "there is no *haikai* [haiku] outside of *makoto*." The word *makoto* is an interesting term that can mean "truth" or "the real" if written 眞, or "sincerity" if written 誠. Onitsura, however, used neither Chinese character, but wrote the word in hiragana as まこと, which could indicate either reading. Both meanings would indicate a background in either or both Confucian or Zen literature. The temple attended by the Uejima family was connected to the Soto Zen sect and it is interesting that one of Onitsura's early noms de plume was Rarari, which in Zen parlance means the sound of a flute. Later in life, he was asked by a Zen abbot, "What is this that you call haiku?" and his response was:

> In the garden,
>   the camellia is blooming
> whitely

and his verse,

> For what reason
>   are the icicles
> some long, some short?

brings to mind the Zen phrase,

> In the scenery of spring, there is not high or low; the flow-
> ering branches are of themselves, some short, some long.

Onitsura would have been familiar with two very familiar Confucian statements: "No twisted thoughts," Confucius' description of classical Chinese poetry; and "Sincerity is the way of Heaven. Sincerity is the path of man. Sincerity hits the mark without effort, and gains effect without thought."

Whatever his influences, Onitsura advocated the commonplace, simplicity and the use of colloquial expressions in haiku in order to be founded in *makoto*. In one of his essays, he wrote,

> The way of haikai seems to resemble shallow, but is deep; it seems to be easy, but is difficult to transmit. The beginner goes from the shallow to the deep; but haven't I heard that when he "arrives," he is back to the shallow?[1]

> The bush warbler chirping,
>   its little mouth
> open.

---

1. Fukuda Iwao, *Onitsura kushu/hitorigoto*.

❧ ❧ ❧

Haiku by Onitsura

New Year's Day;
    the wind from long ago
blowing through the pines.

大旦むかし吹にし松の風
Oo-ashita mukashi fuki ni shi matsu no kaze

Birds playing
    on the budding willow;
a remaining chill.

芽柳の遊ぶ鳥まだ寒げなり
Meyanagi no asobu tori mada samuge nari

Was it a nightingale
    that pooped on a branch
of the plum tree?

鶯か梅の小枝に糞をして
Uguisu ka ume no koeda ni kuso wo shite

Changing lodgings,
    and pulling out nose hair, too;
plum flowers.

宿替えに鼻毛も抜ぬ梅の花
Yadogae ni hanage mo nukinu ume no hana

How melancholy.
    A waking crow
under a hazy moon.

懶はおぼろ烏のねざめ哉
Mono'ui wa oboro karasu no nezame kana

Mountain roses not yet blooming,
    frogs at the bottom
of the streams.

山吹は咲かで蛙は水の底
Yamabuki wa sakade kawazu wa mizu no soko

Night deepens;
    the full sound of the river
at my pillow.

小夜更けて川音高きまくら哉
Sayo fukete kawa'oto takaki makura kana

94

Also delightful
in the dark of night:
stars in the stream.

闇の夜も又おもしろや水の星

Yami no yo mo mata omoshiro ya mizu no hoshi

The cuckoo,
cleaning out my ears
at the mountain pass.

ほととぎす耳すり払ふ峠かな

Hototogisu mimi suriharau touge kana

Chasing away mosquitoes,
my parents' snoring;
a cuckoo.

蚊をよけて親の鼾や時鳥

Ka wo yokete oya no ibiki ya hototogisu

Rustling the lotus,
turtles
in the pond.

さはさはと蓮うごかす池の亀

Sawa sawa to hachisu ugokasu ike no kame

A cool breeze;
filling the empty sky,
the sound of the pines.

涼風や虚空にみちて松の声

Suzukaze ya kokuu ni michite matsu no koe

My heart has almost awakened;
autumn has come,
the sound of the wind.

心略起て秋たつ風の音
Kokoro hobo okite aki tatsu kaze no oto

In the evening,
the spirit of autumn is always
the voices of insects.

宵はいつも秋にかつ気をむしの声
Yoi wa itsumo aki ni kakki wo mushi no koe

Even far from the fields,
blown in with the wind;
voices of insects.

野ばなれや風に吹くるむしのこゑ
Nobanare ya kaze ni fukikuru mushi no koe

The pathos of autumn:
on a moonlit night
the crow is always cawing.

秋はものの月夜烏はいつも鳴く
Aki wa mono no tsukiyo karasu wa itsumo naku

Though I'm called an idler and a fool,
alone, it grows late
admiring the moon.

愚痴愚痴と独に更ける月見哉
Guchi guchi to hitori ni fukeru tsukimi kana

Crossing the river,
　　going on with red feet;
　the withered willows.

川越て赤き足ゆく枯柳

Kawa koete akaki ashi yuku kareyanagi

The voice of the winter storm
　how it resembled
　my thoughts at night.

木がらしの音も似ぬ夜のおもひ哉

Kogarashi no oto mo ninu yo no omoi kana

Waking up
　　with cold knees
　in the Kiso.

膝がしらつめたい木曽の寝覚哉

Hizagashira tsumetai kiso no nezame kana

There is nothing
　　worse for people
　than intelligence.

人間に知恵ほどわるい物はなし

Ningen ni chie hodo warui mono wa nashi

If it blows, let it blow;
　I bought a comb.
　The autumn wind.

吹ばふけ櫛を買たに秋の風

Fukaba fuke kushi wo kouta ni aki no kaze

MIURA CHORA
(1729–1780)

MIURA CHORA WAS BORN in the town of Toba, now in Mie Prefecture. His father left the family when Chora was a child; his mother raised and educated her children by herself and never remarried. Chora studied haiku under a country poet, Hyakuyu, but met Buson when the latter was only twenty. Both were great admirers of Basho and his simplicity of style.

At age thirty-four, Chora settled into a small hermitage in Ise Yamada, which he called the Mu'i-an (無為庵), "the hut of non-action," a reference to the ancient Chinese Taoist classic, the *Tao Te Ching*. Later, he traveled to Kii, Edo (modern-day Tokyo) and northern Echigo, meeting with various poets who inspired him to experiment with different poetry styles, and living a colorful life. His indifferent and extravagant character earned him the antipathy of some of the public, but he cared nothing for practicality or worldly affairs and this was reflected in his literary style.[1]

Chora published a number of haiku collections of his own works, including *Hakuto karasu shu* [The white-headed crow], *Waga io* [My Hermitage] and *Chora hokkushu* [A collection of Chora's hokku], all still read today.

He died of leukemia at the age of fifty-one and is buried at the Kotobukiwao-in, a Jodo Buddhist temple in Ise Yamada.

---

1. The *Tao Te Ching* contains the phrases 聖人之道為而不争, which can be translated as "The way of the sage is to act, but not contend," and 為無為, to "act without acting"—in other words, to act without fabrication. This would lead the Taoist philosopher Chuang-tze to advocate a life of "free and easy wandering," an ideal that Chora plainly took to heart.

❧   ❧   ❧

Chora's haiku are clear and simple, yet rich in poetic elegance. He was fond of classic literature, especially *waka* poetry, and a sense of *aware*—the ah-ness of things—permeates his verses.

> Around my hut,
>   only the fallen leaves
> of the nettle tree.

Compare this in mood to a verse by the poet Fujiwara Teika, written some five hundred years earlier:

> Looking all about,
>   there are neither flowers
> nor autumn leaves,
>   only my thatched hut by the bay
> on an autumn evening.

❧   ❧   ❧

Haiku by Chora

> Nighttimes pleasant,
>   the days peaceful;
> spring rain.

夜はうれしく昼は静かや春の雨
Yoru wa ureshiku hiru wa shizuka ya haru no ame

Cold water,
      two rice cakes:
my summer.

冷水にせんべい二枚樗良が夏
Hiyamizu ni sembei nimai chora ga natsu

Longing for the ancient voice
      of the nightingale;
first day of the year.

うぐいすの古声したふ初日かな
Uguisu no furugoe shitau hatsuhi kana

Captivated by the spring
      light on the wings
of birds.

鳥の羽に見そむる春の光かな
Tori no hane ni misomuru haru no hikari kana

The mountain temple;
      no one comes to see the image
of the Buddha's Final Nirvana.

山寺や誰もまゐらぬ涅槃像
Yamadera ya tare mo mairanu nehanzou

The nightingale singing
      just like yesterday
at this time.

鶯の鳴くや昨日の今自分
Uguisu no naku ya kinou no imajibun

The faraway voice
of the nightingale entwined
with the rising sun.

鶯の遠音につるる日の出かな
Uguisu no toone ni tsururu he no de kana

Confused by the flowers,
surprised by the moon:
butterflies!

花に狂ひ月に驚く胡蝶かな
Hana ni kurui tsuki ni odoroku kochou kana

Travelers looking,
then going on; the willow
at the gate.

旅人の見て行く門の柳かな
Tabibito no mite yuku kado no yanagi kana

It has a scent,
but I can't see
my neighbor's plum tree.

匂ひして隣の梅の見へぬかな
Nioi shite tonari no ume no mienu kana

White plum petals,
falling inside
and out of the fence.

白梅や垣の内外こぼれ散る
Shiraume ya kaki no uchisoto kobore chiru

Flowers in all directions;
the capital,
its heart aflutter.

四方の花に心さわがしき都かな
Yomo no hana ni kokoro sawagashiki miyako kana

A cool breeze
in the august forest
of the shrine.

涼風の尊き森の宮居かな
Suzukaze no toutoki mori no miyai kana

How peaceful!
    Rustling and falling together,
the sound of flowers.

静かさや散るにすれあふ花の音
Shizukasa ya chiru ni sureau hana no oto

Toad!
    Move please, so I can plant
the bamboo.

そこのいて竹植ゑさせよ蟇
Soko noite take uesase yo hikigaeru

Time to eat;
    and through the door,
the light of the setting sun.

飯時や戸口に秋の入日影
Meshidoki ya toguchi ni aki no irihi kage

The blowing gale;
    through the grasses and weeds,
today's moon.

嵐吹く草の中より今日の月
Arashi fuku kusa no naka yori kyou no tsuki

Tinted by the morning glories,
    the blowing wind
of autumn.

朝顔に吹きそめてより秋の風
Asagao ni fukisomete yori aki no kaze

The colors and voices of insects
gently spilling
into the grass.

蟲ほろほろ草にこぼるる音色かな
Mushi horohoro kusa ni koboruru neiro kana

A winter moon;
the river wind
sharpening the stones.

冬の月川風岩をけづるかな
Fuyu no tsuki kawakaze iwa wo kezuru kana

Lingering wind
and snow, falling on me
round and about.

風の雪イむ我を降りめぐる
Kaze no yuki tatazumu ware wo furimeguru

Vanishing away,
the moon;
plovers at dawn.

消えてもせむ有明月の濱千鳥
Kiete mo sen ariake tsuki no hama chidori

TAIGU RYOKAN
(1758–1831)

TAIGU RYOKAN WAS BORN in Izumozaki, a village on the Sea of Japan coast in what is now Niigata Prefecture, with the childhood name of Yamamoto Eizo. His father was the village headman and the custodian of the local Shinto shrine; he was also a somewhat well-known haiku poet whose poems were written under the nom de plume I'nan. The boy had an unremarkable education in traditional Japanese and Chinese literature, taught by a Confucian scholar.

At age seventeen, Ryokan suddenly left home and entered a local Zen Buddhist temple. His motivation for doing so is unclear—as the eldest son he would have inherited his father's positions—but one account is that he was deeply shocked at witnessing the beheading of a criminal. During his time at the local temple, he refused to accept any charity or support from his parents, and eventually left to become a disciple of the priest Kokusen and reside in the Entsuji temple in what is now Okayama Prefecture. It was here that he took the name Ryokan (良寛, "Well at Ease").

When Kokusen passed away in 1791, Ryokan left the Entsuji and went on a wandering journey for the next five years. Although he had received the *inka*, the Seal of the Dharma—a formal recognition of enlightenment that allowed him to engage in teaching—he now lived by walking from house to house, begging for food and chanting the sutras, a practice he would follow nearly all of his life.

In 1804, Ryokan settled into a tumbledown hut on the slope of Mount Kugami (in present-day Niigata Prefecture). This hermitage, the Gogo-an, had a leaky roof and walls through which a cold wind whistled in the fall and winter. Nevertheless, Ryokan lived here for thirteen years, begging when the weather was not too inclement, writing poetry in Chinese and Japanese and spending much time playing with the local children. There are a number of stories about his games with children, the most famous concerning *kakurenbo*, hide and go seek. Once, Ryokan hid behind a bale of hay, but after a while the children gave up looking for him and went home. The next morning he was found still hiding by a local housewife, and when she asked what he was doing, he said, "Shhh, they'll find me." This is an example, perhaps, of the reason why he gave himself the name Taigu, "the Great Fool."

Ryokan was known for his simplicity and frugal living. Another famous story is that he came back to his hut one evening to discover that a thief had broken in, and finding nothing else worth stealing, had taken off with Ryokan's bedding. Feeling sorry that the thief had gone to such trouble for only a used futon, he wished that he might have given the man the beautiful moon that night:

> Left behind
> by the thief,
> the moon in the window.

As he grew older and his health declined, Ryokan moved in 1831 to a residence in the grounds of the Otogo shrine and later into a storehouse owned by his patron, Kimura Motoemon. In his final years, he was cared for by a young nun, Teishin, with whom he had exchanged haiku and affection. Before he died, Teishin asked for a death poem, and he wrote:

> Showing the backside,
> showing the front;
> falling autumn leaves.

He is said to have passed away quietly seated in meditation.

❧   ❧   ❧

Ryokan's art was for the most part classical Japanese and Chinese poetry, and calligraphy, but he always retained his own individual style and evaded the reputation of "poet" or "calligrapher." He famously wrote:

> Who says my poetry is poetry?
> My poetry is not poetry.
> The person who knows that my poetry is not poetry,
> Is someone I can talk with about poetry.

He admired the T'ang dynasty Chinese poet Han Shan and, although without the eccentricity of that poet, wrote with a similar simplicity and unabashed approach to everyday life. Living alone, he was not immune to human feelings:

> On rainy days,
> the monk Ryokan
> feels sad.

And, although alcohol was formally proscribed by Buddhism, Ryokan, like other Zen monks, often enjoyed one or two or three cups of saké.

Lightly drunk,
     my footsteps also light;
  a spring breeze.

Never having made or published a collection of his own poems, it was the nun Teishin who gathered together what she could along with stories of his life in a work entitled *Hachisu no tsuyu* [Dew on the lotus], some five years after his passing.

❧   ❧   ❧

Haiku by Ryokan

All the world
    has become the flowers
  of the cherry.

世の中はさくらの花になりにけり
Yo no naka wa sakura no hana ni narinikeri

A nightingale;
    to even a hundred people,
  it pays no attention.

鶯や百人ながら気がつかず
Uguisu ya hyakunin nagara ki ga tsukazu

A new pond,
    a fog jumps in;
  no sound at all.

新池や蛙とびこむ音もなし
Araike ya kawazu tobikomu oto mo nashi

Since it's all the same,
I'll sleep one night
under the flowers.

同じくば花の下にて一とよ寝む
Onajikuba hana no moto nite hitoyo nen

If I don't come today,
they'll fall tomorrow;
plum blossoms.

けふ来ずばあすは散りなむ梅の花
Kyo kozuba asu wa chirinan ume no hana

I'm a little drunk,
so I'm treading lightly;
the spring wind.

ほろ酔いのあしもと軽し春のかぜ
Horoyoi no ashimoto karoshi haru no kaze

The mountain villages
have become
the croaking of frogs.

やま里は蛙の声になりにけり
Yamazato wa kawazu no koe ni nari ni keri

Awakened from dreams
by the nightingale;
time for breakfast!

鶯にゆめさまされし朝げかな
Uguisu ni yume samasareshi asage kana

In the begging bowl,
tomorrow's rice;
the evening cool.

鉄鉢に明日の米あり夕涼

Teppachi ni asu no kome ari yuusuzumi

Mixed in with the sound
of scrubbing the pot;
frogs in the rain.

なべみがくおとにまぎるる雨蛙

Nabe migaku oto ni magiruru amegaeru

A place to get drunk
and lie down:
lotus flowers.

酔ひ臥しのところはここに蓮の花

Yoifushi no tokoro wa koko ni hasu no hana

Alone in an empty house,
how lonely;
falling pine needles.

留守の戸にひとり淋しき散り松葉
Rusu no to ni hitori sabishiki chiri matsuba

I'd like to take it back
to my home;
the bird on the lotus.

わが宿へつれて行きたし蓮に鳥
Waga yado e tsurete yukitashi hasu ni tori

How I appear?
Standing alone
in the autumn wind.

あきかぜに独り立ちたる姿かな
Akikaze ni hotori tachitaru sugata kana

In the dark of night,
my garden:
the chirping of insects.

宵闇や前栽はただ虫の声
Yoi yami ya senzai wa tada mushi no koe

Just like the persimmons,
my testicles are cold
in the autumn wind.

柿もぎのきんたまさむし秋の風
Kakimogi no kintama samushi aki no kaze

Left behind
by the thief,
the moon in the window.

ぬす人に取りのこされし窓の月
Nusubito ni torinokosareshi mado no tsuki

Rain leaking,
there's another place to sleep;
the cold!

雨もりやまた寝るとこのさむさかな
Amamori ya mata neru tokoro no samusa kana

Little birds gathering
in the brushwood fence;
a morning of snow.

柴垣に小鳥あつまるゆきのあさ
Shibagaki ni kotori atsumaru yuki no asa

The wind blows in
just enough for kindling;
autumn leaves.

焚くほどは風がもてくる落葉かな
Taku hodo wa kaze ga mote kuru ochiba kana

First winter rain;
how interesting,
this mountain with no name.

初時雨名もなき山のおもしろき
Hatsushigure na mo naki yama no omoshiroki

Every day, every day,
    winter rains falling;
  a man gets old.

日々日々に時雨の降れば人老いぬ
Hibi hibi ni shigure no fureba hito oinu

Dewdrops
    on the brushwood door;
  this morning's dawn.

柴の戸につゆのたまりや今朝のあさ
Shiba no to ni tsuyu no tamari ya kesa no asa

On rainy days,
    he feels pathetic;
  the monk Ryokan.

雨の降る日はあはれなり良寛坊
Ame no furu hi wa aware nari ryoukanbo

INOUE SEIGETSU
(1822–1887)

INOUE SEIGETSU WAS BORN in the town of Nagaoka in what is now Niigata Prefecture, the son of a warrior family (or possibly of sword sharpeners) who lost their samurai status with the Meiji Restoration in 1868 and turned to farming. Details of his early life are unclear, but he seems to have left for Edo (modern-day Tokyo) at age eighteen, then spent a life of wandering.

According to most accounts, Seigetsu "suddenly" appeared in the Ina Valley at about age forty and made this his pied-à-terre for the rest of his life. He was considered highly educated and an expert at calligraphy by the local people of the area, which had been a center of learning since ancient times. Thus he was welcomed by the wealthier patrons of the arts and visited the homes of poets and scholars, tutoring haiku groups and teaching Confucianism. He was more often than not happy to be recompensed with saké and a meal, and in some cases was given board at the homes of his patrons. His favorite way of saying thanks, especially for the gift of saké—or goodbye, or congratulations—was *senryo, senryo* (千両, 千両), literally " a thousand pieces of gold."

Eventually, however, Seigetsu became little more than an entertaining beggar in dirty, flea-infested robes. The wealthy and educated men of the area still enjoyed his company and teaching, but the women found his filthiness abhorrent and children were afraid of him. According to a contemporary, a child at the time:

> When I was about ten years old, five or six friends were on the way home from elementary school, and unexpectedly noticed Seigetsu's figure from the back as he tottered

along. We decided that we would throw stones and break the gourd that swung hanging from his hip [. . .] Bad boys that we were, we became irritated when we missed and threw more and more stones. But one of them, aimed or not, hit the back of his head and drew blood. Seigetsu, however, did not turn around or alter his gait. I became very frightened and ran away, as did the other boys. When I returned home about dusk, Seigetsu was there drinking saké. At dinner I heard that my aunt had applied some medicine to his wound, and I got nervous, but he had said nothing about our mischief. The next day when I told the story to an upperclassman at school, he said, "Seigetsu is immortal and insensitive to pain."

Seigetsu seemed to embody the quote from Confucius, "No twisted thoughts," and harbored no resentments. In his compassion for even the smallest creatures, when washing his clothes he would take out the fleas and line them up on the rocks beside the stream. If dogs challenged him in the street, he would remain calm and walk on until the dogs lost interest and went away

Such a precarious lifestyle eventually took its toll and Seigetsu's health began to decline. In December of 1886, he collapsed in a rice field in the mountains and was found covered with mud and filth. Unable to speak or move, he was gently placed on a rain shutter and taken back to the home of a villager. On March 10 of the following year, he was offered a writing brush and paper and was asked to write a *jisei*, or death poem. He wrote:

> Somewhere in the mist,
> I hear
> the call of a crane.

Then, with a sip of potato wine, he passed away.

❦   ❦   ❦

Seigetsu wrote some 1,700 verses. He admired Basho and was influenced by the latter's *Narrow Road to the Deep North*, but had his own personal style. Like Shiki, he was critical of the Basho school of haiku after the latter's passing. In his *Haikai gazoku den* [Transmission of the refined and vulgar in haiku], he wrote,

> Though your words should be the common language, your heart should not fall short of [classical] Chinese and Japanese poetry. Which means that you should always aim towards grace and refinement. The form of your verses should be like flowing water: smooth and tranquil. You should not make them crooked and stiff like a tree. You should not think of making a good verse; just make it without effort [. . .] If your subject is mundane, make it with elegance; if the subject is elegant, garnish it with the commonplace.

> The prostitute has a taste
> for morning saké;
> autumn leaves.

Saké and the saké shop were two of his favorite subjects:

> No shortcut
> to the saké shop;
> year's end.

> Some more than others,
> drunk on return from viewing
> autumn leaves.

Seigetsu is better known in Japan than in the West. There is no mention of him in R. H. Blyth's six volumes of work on haiku, yet he had a great influence on writer Akutagawa Ryunosuke and the poets Santoka, Seisensui and Hosai. In Japan, "complete" collections of his work were published in 1930 and 1974 and continue to be reprinted today. In 2015, the Japanese movie *Hokaibito: Ina no Seigetsu* about Seigetsu, was shown at the Expo Milano in Italy.

❧   ❧   ❧

Haiku by Seigetsu

Throughout the morning,
napping off and on;
a night of fleas and no sleep.

朝の間や蚤に寝ぬ夜の仮枕
Asa no ma ya nomi ni nenu yo no karimakura

Stuffed in my lunchbox,
millet brandy!
In the shade of young leaves.

重づめに泡盛酒や若葉蔭
Juuzume ni awamori sake ya wakaba kage

An October peach!
And not worm-eaten!
On the path to the bath.

虫食ぬ十月桃や温泉の径
Mushi kuwanu juugatsutou ya yu no komichi

Year after year,
    the way home forgotten;
a flowery spring.

年々や家路忘れて花の春
Toshidoshi ya ieji wasurete hana no haru

Beginning autumn;
    putting strength into their cries,
cicadas.

秋立や声に力を入れる蝉
Aki tatsu ya koe ni chikara wo ireru semi

Right up to today,
    no sins committed,
    three whole days.

今日までは罪も作らず三ヶ日
Kyou made wa tsumi mo tsukurazu mikkahi

Saké tasting;
    tilting my head to one side in judgment:
lingering summer heat.

きき酒に小首かたげる残暑かな
Kikizake ni kokubi katageru zansho kana

First dawn of the New Year;
    in my mind,
    a day of ladling saké.

初空を心に酒をくむ日かな
Hatsuzora wo kokoro ni sake wo kumu hi kana

At midday
    this walk doesn't go as planned;
the heat!

日も中は道はかどらぬ暑さかな
Hi mo naka wa michi hakadoranu atsusa kana

Departing autumn;
    one little pleasure?
Plenty of saké.

行秋や酒沢山を小楽しみ
Yuku aki ya sake takusan wo kotanoshimi

Gathering firewood,
    a fox's luck:[1]
matsutake!

松茸や薪拾ひの狐福
Matsutake ya takigi hiroi no kitsune fuku

On a day the mountain laughs,[2]
    in the detached room,
a minor drinking bout.

山笑ふ日や放れ家の小酒盛
Yama warau hi ya hanareya no kozakamori

---

1. Unexpected good luck
2. A Japanese saying has it that the mountains laugh in the spring, drip in the summer, adorn themselves in autumn and sleep in winter.

White chrysanthemums!
No hiding in the dark:
the saké shop.

白菊や闇にかくれのなき酒屋

Shiragiku ya yami ni kakure no naki sakaya

No shortcut
to the saké shop;
year's end.

帘に近道のなし年の暮

Sakabayashi ni chikamichi no nashi toshi no kure

Not knowing what will happen
to me tomorrow, what better pleasure!
Saké under the flowers.

翌日しらぬ身の楽しみや花に酒

Asu shiranu mi no tanoshimi ya hana ni sake

Spring rain;
elbow for a pillow,
just as I please.

春雨や心のままのひじ枕

Harusame ya kokoro no mama no hijimakura

The prostitute has a taste
for morning saké;
autumn leaves.

傾城の朝酒たしむ紅葉かな

Keisei no asazake tashimu momiji kana

Ignoring the fact that I need
to sleep;
cats in spring.

ねたるべき事も忘れて春の猫

Netarubeki koto mo wasurete haru no neko

In the hazy light
of the bedroom;
a faraway frog.

閨の灯の朧になりて遠蛙

Neya no akari no oboro ni narite too kawazu

Cloudy skies;
hearing their first croaks:
frogs at night.

空の曇り蛙の初音聞く夜かな

Sora no kumori kawazu no hatsune kiku yo kana

The hot spring did the trick;
taking the roundabout way home.
Autumn leaves.

温泉の利きて廻り道する紅葉かな

Yu no kikite mawarimichi suru momiji kana

First snow!
Even with a little saké,
flowers bloom in the heart.

初雪や小半酒も花ごころ

Hatsu yuki ya konakarazake mo hanagokoro

NATSUME SOSEKI

(1867–1916)

NATSUME SOSEKI IS BEST KNOWN as a novelist, author of the well-known works *I am a Cat*, *Botchan* and *Kokoro*, but he was also a talented and productive writer of both haiku and Chinese poetry.

Born Natsume Kin'nosuke in what is now the Shinjuku area of Tokyo, he was a late and unexpected child of an already large family and was thought of as superfluous by his father, a man who had been a ward chief in Tokyo but who lost that position with the Meiji Restoration of 1868. The family was not a wealthy one and the infant Kin'nosuke was adopted in that year by a childless couple, who divorced when he was nine, and he was returned to his original home. His father continued to treat him with little enthusiasm, a factor that may have contributed to his paranoia and depression later on.

Kin'nosuke was an excellent student and studied Chinese and Japanese literature in middle school. Accepted to the prestigious Tokyo Imperial University in 1881, he was encouraged to study engineering by his family, but quickly transferred to the Department of Literature. It was there that he met the poet Masaoka Shiki, who encouraged him in his literary studies and tutored him in haiku. In 1896, he left Tokyo and moved to Matsuyama, where Shiki, Kyoshi and Hekigodo lived, taught at a local high school, published haiku and poems in Chinese in newspapers and periodicals and began using the name Soseki. A year later, he took another teaching job in Kumamoto, where he had an arranged marriage.

In 1900, Soseki was awarded a scholarship to study English at the University of London for two years. The amount was so meager, however, that he soon transferred to a less expensive school, but devoted himself to his studies of eighteenth-century English literature.

By all accounts, Soseki's sojourn in London was a miserable one, in which he had almost no social life and became more and more withdrawn. In the two years there, he changed residences four times, always searching for less expensive places to live. His last and happiest location was a house he shared with a Ms Priscilla Leale and her sister, with whom he got along quite well. The sisters worried about Soseki's progressive paranoia, encouraged him to become more sociable and to try bicycle riding as a way of getting some fresh air. Concerning the latter, he wrote:

> Adjusting my buttocks,
> I get on
> the bicycle.

He had continued a correspondence with Shiki during this time, sending him haiku and letters concerning his lonely life.

In 1903, Soseki returned to Tokyo and served four years as a lecturer in English literature at his former university, where he replaced the Irish writer, Lafcadio Hearn. It was during this time that Kyoshi requested him to write something for the literary magazine, *Hototogisu*, and Soseki produced a short story, *I Am a Cat*. Kyoshi suggested some revisions and the result was its publication in 1905. This time, Kyoshi was impressed, and chapters were added through 1907. It was published as a single book in 1911. With the completion of the last chapter, Soseki resigned his position at the university and became the literary editor for the *Asahi Shimbun* newspaper, a position he would hold until his death from a stomach ulcer in 1916.

❧   ❧   ❧

As a child, Soseki and his friends loved *rakugo*, comic recitations by professional storytellers, and this can be detected at times in both his prose and haiku. Two examples might be the previously quoted verse on his attempt at bicycle riding and perhaps the following:

> A cuckoo!
> half-finished in the outhouse,
> I was unable to leave.

And though he was encouraged and critiqued by Shiki to practice *shasei*, or describing a living situation, not unlike a photograph, there are often touches of melancholy in Soseki's verses that express more of his inner feelings than his outer vision. If we can guess from his numerous references to temples and priests, he may have also been influenced by Buddhism's teachings on contemplation and compassion:

> Autumn flies;
> catching them,
> letting them go.

To which could be added humor:

> Just a little
> jealous of
> the Panama hat.

Throughout his life, Soseki wrote voluminous letters, essays, Chinese poetry, linked verse and haiku. There are entire books consisting of his correspondence with Shiki right up to the latter's death in 1902. He was, above all, a literary man whose books are reprinted in Japan almost yearly, and whose portrait adorned the one thousand yen note until 2004. Yet, for all his success and fame, one feels a certain sadness and loneliness to his life which began in his youth and from which he never recovered. One of his final verses reads:

> Ask the wind:
>   which leaf will be
> the first to fall.

※   ※   ※

Haiku by Soseki

> Hunting for fireflies,
>   I fall
> into a creek.

蛍狩りわれを小川に落しけり
Hotarugari ware wo ogawa no ochishikeri

> During the priest's break
>   at the wake;
> a grasshopper!

通夜僧の経を絶間やきりぎりす
Tsuya sou no kyou wo taema ya kirigirisu

Gathering her ashes;
this, too, the end
of a beauty.

骸骨やこれも美人のなれの果
Gaikotsu ya kore mo bijin no nare no hate

The year's first dream!
I didn't pick up money,
but didn't die either.

初夢や金も拾はず死にもせず
Hatsu yume ya kane mo hirowazu shini mo sezu

The winter mountain,
unnoticed;
people passing by.

冬の山人通ふとも見えざりき
Fuyu no yama hito kayou tomo miezariki

Clouds come,
clouds go; autumn leaves
in the waterfall.

雲来り雲去る瀑の紅葉かな
Kumo kitari kumo saru taki no momiji kana

One star visible;
unable to sleep,
a frosty night.

星一つ見えて寝られぬ霜夜哉
Hoshi hitotsu miete nerarenu shimoyo kana

The main temple:
> seventy-two square feet
of cold!

本堂は十八間の寒さ哉
Hondou wa juuhachi ken no samusa kana

Riding along,
> my horse shits
on the wild chrysanthemums.

乗りながら馬の糞する野菊哉
Norinagara uma no fun suru nogiku kana

Beating the mokugyo,[1]
> it disgorges
midday's mosquitoes.

叩かれて昼の蚊を吐く木魚哉
Tatakarete hiru no ka wo haku mokugyo kana

A long day;
> infecting each other with yawns,
we part.

永き日や欠伸うつして別れ行く
Nagaki hi ya akubi utsushite wakare yuku

---

1. *Mokugyo*: a sort of fish-shaped wooden drum with an opening in the front. Used to beat time to the recitation of sutras.

Drawing swords in iai,[2]
　　they dodge each other
　　with the swiftness of swallows.

居合ぬけば燕ひらりと身をかわす
Iai nukeba tsubame hirari to mi wo kawasu

In this transient world,
　　how will I become a monk?
　　An afternoon nap.

うき世いかに坊主となりて昼寝する
Ukiyo ikani bouzu to narite hirune suru

---

2. Iai: a martial art in which participants practice drawing swords as if in
actual combat.

A place in the sun;
I feel like
a ripe persimmon.

日あたりや熟柿のごとき心地あり

Hiatari ya jukushi no gotoki kokochi ari

Setting its stout bottom
down,
the pumpkin.

どつしりと尻を据えたる南瓜かな

Dosshiri to shiri wo suetaru kabocha kana

Squatting naked
at the pool:
our teacher.

裸体なる先生胡座す水泳所

Ratai naru sensei koza su sui'eisho

Crickets, suddenly
start chirping, suddenly
stop.

蟬のふと鳴き出しぬ鳴きやみぬ

Koorogi no futo nakidashinu nakiyaminu

The departing year;
the cat curled up
on my lap.

行く年や猫うずくまる膝の上

Yuku toshi ya neko uzukumaru hiza no ue

Out on a journey
with no excuses;
end of the year.

旅にして申訳なく暮るる年
Tabi ni shite moushiwake naku kururu toshi

Passing through the withered moor
without a lamp;
the cold!

無提灯で枯野を通る寒さ哉
Muchouchin de kareno wo tooru samusa kana

Feeding on flowers.
the nightingale's poop
should be red, too.

花食まば鶯の糞も赤からん
Hana hamaba uguisu no fun mo akaran

If you should ask
the enlightened road of glistening dew,
it is morning, it is night.

白露に悟道を問えば朝な友な
Shiratsuyu ni godou wo toeba asa na yuu na

KAWAHIGASHI HEKIGODO
(1873–1937)

KAWAHIGASHI HEKIGODO declared early on that a rigid attention to the traditional formats of haiku—followed since the time of Basho—would dilute the poet's impressions and the vitality of the Japanese language. Thus, the compositional pattern of 7-5-7 syllables and the inclusion of a word indicating the season were thrown overboard to create a movement that is often referred to as "New Haiku." The following are two examples, the originals of which contain twenty-six and twenty-five syllables respectively:

> Recently his wife has died;
>> loading the greens, loading
>> the long onions,
> the greengrocer and his daughter.

> In the rear there are rice fields.
>> and in the corner
>> of the house,
> drying lotuses.

The son of a Confucian scholar, Hekigodo received a classical education and had broad interests. He learned to play baseball—which would eventually become the unofficial national sport of Japan—from the poet Shiki. He also enjoyed mountain climbing, and traveled extensively in Japan, China, Europe and North America. He was also an extraordinary calligrapher, and carried difficult Noh drama librettos with him to chant when traveling.

Hekigodo worked for newspapers throughout his life, and wrote journals and essays. He married at the age of twenty-eight and, despite his frequent travels and mountain climbing, seemed to cherish his family life, even adopting the children of two of his siblings.

> Boiling daikon;
> dinner together
> with the children.

> Knee to knee,
> the moon shines in;
> refreshingly cool.

> A winter night;
> the children's sleeping breath, my breath
> together.

The haiku poet Takahama Kyoshi, whom Hekigodo had known from an early age, was a close friend and colleague and, like Hekigodo, was devoted to Shiki. Together they worked on the haiku magazine *Hototogisu*, but soon after Shiki's death, Hekigodo and Kyoshi parted ways, as Kyoshi returned to more conservative views on haiku.

Hekigodo's taste for travel seems to have begun at the age of nineteen when he traveled the Kiso Road, a favorite of many poets from early times. His first serious trip through Japan, however, would be a four-month trip in 1906 at the age of thirty-four which was then published as a travelogue in the *Nippon* newspaper. These travels throughout the country continued for the next number of years, but in 1920, at the age of forty-eight, he sailed out of Kobe for Shanghai, Hong Kong, Singapore, Genoa, Rome, Venice, Milan, Florence, Paris, Berlin, London,

Washington DC, Chicago and San Francisco, then returning to Yokohama. The following year, he once again traveled through the Orient, Europe and North America; and he continued his journeys—both domestic and foreign—until a year before his death. It is sometimes said that Hekigodo's talent in haiku waned in his latter years, and that some of disciples deserted him. But it seems more likely that he was increasingly caught up in his travels and the books he would write about them. His *Sanzenri* [Three thousand leagues], for example, runs to four volumes.

Finally, in January of 1937, he celebrated the establishment of a new residence with a number of friends, but at the end of the month was taken to a hospital on suspicion of having contracted typhoid fever. He passed away from complications of blood poisoning on February 1.

Hekigodo was taught the Chinese classics from the age of five, and said that he was never without a libretto of one Noh play or another. While in Europe, he attended a performance of Wagner's opera *Parsifal* and found it completely captivating. Still, in his haiku, we find something quite earthy and human about this cultured and elegant man:

> On a journey,
>   lunch with saké!
> and peaches!

> Forgiven for being drunk,
>   I sit up straight
> at the brazier.

Haiku by Hekigodo

Finding lodging in the rain;
when the rain clears,
dragonflies!

雨に泊れば雨は晴れたる蜻蛉かな
Ame ni tomareba ame wa haretaru tonbo kana

This road:
all we can depend on;
the withered moor.

この道に寄る外はなき枯野かな
Kono michi ni yoru hoka wa naki kareno kana

Faraway fireworks
making a noise, then
nothing.

遠花火音して何もなかりけり
Toohanabi oto shite nanimo nakarikeri

Once again
I'm alone;
early summer rain.

又ただの一人になりぬさみだれん
Mata tada no hitori ni narinu samidaren

A wooden bathtub,
a couple enters in;
a cold night, I guess.

据え風呂に二人入りこむ夜寒かな
Sueburo ni futari irikomu yosamu kana

Throughout the city,
crows watching people;
deepening autumn.

市中鴉人を見る秋の暮
Shichuu karasu hito wo miru aki no kure

Slipping and falling
in the pampas grass,
the firefly.

すべり落つる薄の中の蛍かな
Suberi otsuru susuki no naka no hotaru kana

Chasing around, running away;
how clever the crows
on the withered moor.

追ふて逃げる鴉かしこき枯野哉
Oute nigeru karasu kashikoki kareno kana

Taking lodging from the downpour,
then forgetting about the rain;
at the window, fireflies!

雨宿りして雨忘れ窓蛍哉
Ameyadori shite ame wasure mado hotaru kana

Rinsing the tub
in the evening;
the voices of insects.

夜ながら盥すすぎや虫の声
Yo nagara tarai susugi ya mushi no koe

The sweet potato vine
crawling into the street;
autumn wind.

秋風や道に這ひ出るいもの蔓
Aki kaze ya michi ni haideru imo no tsuru

Early summer rain;
the school on vacation
in a small village.

五月雨に学校やすむ小村かな
Samidare ni gakkou yasumu komura kana

The destitute temple
in the cold woods, burned down;
the monk absent.

寒林の貧寺焼けたり僧の留守
Kanrin no mazutera yaketari sou no rusu

The dirty lower leaves
of the bush clover;
the path of the toad.

萩の下葉の汚れたるに蟇の這出でつ
Hagi no shitaba no yogoretaru ni hiki no haidetsu

Continuing to drink saké,
among the flowers, what foolishness:
a hangover.

花に酒居つづけの愚や二日酔
Hana ni sake itsuzuke no gu ya futsukayoi

Setting down the saké,
tears of old age;
the round wooden brazier.

酒を置いて老の涙の火桶かな
Sake wo oite oi no namida no hioke kana

Cold at night.
hearing human voices;
the forest temple.

夜を寒み人語聞えて森の寺
Yo wo samumi jingo kikoete mori no tera

Neat and clean,
    a summer book;
no dust.

清浄と夏書の一間塵もなし
Shoujou to gekaki no hitoma chiri mo nashi

Praying for rain;
    the humble face, too,
praying, praying.

雨乞ひの下賤の顔も祈りけり
Amagoi no gesen no kao mo inorikeri

Wreaking havoc,
    chased by wasps,
off I go!

あらすごの熊蜂に追はれ逃げにけり
Arasugo no kumahachi ni oware nigenikeri

The packhorse passing by,
    dropping shit
in the northern wind.

北風に糞落し行く荷馬かな
Kita kaze ni fun otoshiyuku niuma kana

Crossing over water
    spilt from the morning glory;
a mouse!

朝顔の出水を渡る鼠かな
Asagao no demizu wo wataru nezumi kana

TAKAHAMA KYOSHI
(1874–1959)

TAKAHAMA KYOSHI WAS BORN in Matsuyama City. His father, Ikeuchi Masatada, had been a samurai, a sword master, a strong swimmer and an avid follower of Noh drama, but with the Meiji Restoration in 1868 which abolished the old feudal system, he lost his status, moved to the countryside and took up farming. Thus, as a young child, Kyoshi was exposed to both the beauty of nature and the high culture of Japan. His mother, also of a samurai family, was educated in the Chinese classics and was a talented calligrapher. In high school, his friend Hekigodo introduced him to the poet Shiki, to whom he would remain devoted all his life. At the age of nine, he received an inheritance from his grandmother and took her surname, Takahama.

In 1894, Kyoshi moved to Tokyo and eventually became an editor for the literary magazine, *Nihonjin*. He was also writing and submitting his own haiku and, along with Hekigodo, began dropping the traditional haiku syllable count of 5-7-5 and the *kigo*, or season word. In 1898, he became the editor of another literary magazine, *Hototogisu*, the position formerly held by Shiki, and moved its headquarters from Matsuyama to Tokyo. At this juncture, Kyoshi returned to the traditional structures of haiku and so began a long literary feud with Hekigodo, which would continue until the latter's death. His affection for his old friend never waned, however, and this he expressed in a memorial verse:

> We are, for example,
>   like two spinning tops
>   banging into each other.

Kyoshi began to write novels in 1908, possibly under the influence of his friend, Natsume Soseki, and, inheriting a love of Noh drama from his father, also wrote some plays.

He continued to write novels, haiku and essays on haiku throughout his life. As busy as he was with literary matters, he also took pleasure and inspiration in travel, though perhaps not nearly so much as Hekigodo, Basho or Buson. One of his favorite journeys, like the others, seems to have been along the Kiso Road.

> Evening clouds for early summer rains
> come quickly;
> a village in the Kiso.

In 1910, he moved to the seaside town of Kamakura, near Tokyo, where he would remain until his passing at the age of eighty-five.

❧   ❧   ❧

Kyoshi emphasized Shiki's insistence on *shasei*, or describing reality, and in this way did not dwell on beauty or the mysterious. There are no particular "aha" moments in his verse such as the sound of water when a frog jumps into a pond. Nature (reality) is here, and we should see it simply as it is.

> Watching a snake
> leaving its hole:
> a crow.

> Birds chirping,
> swelling, then ending,
> then quiet.

He was, however, a devout Buddhist of the Amidist sect, which holds that all nature is sentient and thus contains the Buddha nature.

> The mountain butterfly,
>   as lovely as
> the Buddha.

> An autumn mosquito
>   has come inside,
> the strict temple rules.

The temple prohibition of taking life, or the rule of sitting absolutely still during meditation? And like Saint Francis, it is the believer's duty to preach to all beings.

> The old monk
>   scolds the snake
> and sends it on its way.

Kyoshi had a great influence on later poets, as did his friend and rival Hekigodo. The division of haiku styles—Kyoshi's more classic form and Hekigodo's "New Haiku," which drops the traditional syllable count of 5-7-5 and the season word—has continued to this day. Kyoshi was considered to be a little rough around the edges, perhaps too austere, yet he was an admired teacher, and seems to have been very popular among women haiku poets. He was awarded the Order of Culture by the Japanese government in 1954 and, posthumously, the Order of the Sacred Treasure, First Class. He is buried at the Jufukuji, a Rinzai Zen temple in Kamakura.

❧   ❧   ❧

Haiku by Kyoshi

The snake slithered away,
     but in the grass, the eyes that stared at me
remained.

蛇逃げて我を見し眼の草に残る
Hebi nigete ware wo mishime no kusa ni nokoru

A sudden shower
          on the straw rain hat
          stolen from the scarecrow.

盗んだる案山子の笠に雨急なり
Nusundaru kakashi no kasa ni ame kyuu nari

This spring, too,
          when I thought to travel,
          has come to an end.

旅せんと思ひし春も暮れにけり
Tabi sen to omoishi haru mo kure ni keri

Cutting the peony,
          there was nothing at all left
     in the garden.

牡丹切つて庭にものなくなりにけり
Botan kitte niwa ni mono naku nari ni keri

The autumn wind!
In my heart,
how many mountains and rivers.

秋風や心のなかの幾山河
Aki kaze ya kokoro no naka no ikusanga

Birds chirping;
swelling, then ending,
then quiet.

囀の高まり終わり静まりぬ
Saezuri no takamari owari shizumarinu

Catching up with them,
sending them on;
traveling alone in spring.

おひつくもおくるるも春の旅一人
Oitsuku mo okururu mo haru no tabi hitori

Watching the snake
leaving its hole;
a crow!

穴を出る蛇を見て居る鴉かな
Ana wo deru hebi wo mite iru karasu kana

Stepping along the planks,
the squishing of spring
mud.

板踏めば春泥こたへ動きけり
Ita fumeba shundei kotae ugokikeri

In the mountain temple,
incense burning;
the long day.

山寺に線香もゆる日永かな
Yamadera ni senko moyuru hinaga kana

A spring night
on my desk,
my elbow for a pillow.

春の夜や机の上の肱まくら
Haru no yo ya tsukue no ue no hiji makura

Closing the rain shutters,
now heard from far away,
the frogs!

雨戸たてて遠くなりたる蛙かな
Amado tatete toku naritaru kawazu kana

Forgetting
that I'm on a journey;
sleeping late.

旅にあることも忘れて朝寝かな
Tabi ni aru koto mo wasurete asane kana

Evening clouds for early summer rains
come quickly;
a village in the Kiso.

五月雨の夕雲早し木曽の里
Samidare no yugumo hayashi Kiso no sato

Going back and forth,
        not even stepping on them:
toads.

往来に踏まれもせずに蟇
Ourai ni fumaremosezu ni hikigaeru

In a lodging you've gotten used to,
        even the mosquitoes
    are interesting.

住みなれし宿なれば蚊もおもしろや
Suminareshi yado nareba ka mo omoshiro ya

The old monk
        scolds the snake
    and drives it away.

老僧の蛇を叱りて追ひにけり
Roso no hebi wo shikarite oinikeri

An autumn mosquito
    has come inside;
    the strict temple rules.[1]

秋の蚊の居りてけはしき寺法かな
Aki no ka no irite kewashiki jiho kana

---

1. Could refer to the Buddhist prohibition against taking life or to the rule of sitting absolutely still during meditation.

An autumnal breeze;
    all things in my view
are haiku.

秋風や眼中のもの皆俳句
Akikaze ya ganchu no mono mina haiku

Hurrying along
    from teahouse to teahouse;
early winter rains

時雨るると茶屋から茶屋へ小走りに
Shigururu to chaya kara chaya e kobashiri ni

Winter seclusion;
    even my beard,
grown just a little?

冬籠髯でも少しはやそうか
Fuyugormori hige demo sukoshi hayaso ka

Like ashes, my memory
    is just there;
end of the year.

灰の如き記憶ただあり年暮るる
Hai no gotoki kioku tada ari toshi kururu

Having been scolded,
    I crawled in
under the covers.

叱られてもぐりこんだる蒲団かな
Shikararete mogurikondaru futon kana

TANEDA SANTOKA

(1882–1940)

TANEDA SANTOKA WAS BORN in the Hachioji neighborhood of what is now the city of Hofu, near the southwestern tip of the island of Honshu. His family owned a great deal of land and it was said they could walk to the train station without stepping on other people's property. His father, Takejiro, was a gregarious man who did not indulge in saké, but rather favored courtesans. His mother, Fusa, was loving, but high-strung, and drowned herself in the family well during an episode of her husband's "travels" with a geisha when Santoka was ten years old. The child saw his mother's body being taken from the well, an event from which he never recovered; later, in his travels as an adult, he took his mother's mortuary tablet with him wherever he went.

Santoka was literarily minded from the time of his teens, attended the prestigious Waseda University, but withdrew after two years, ostensibly because of "neurasthenia," but more likely because of his father's mismanagement of funds. Two years later, when Santoka was twenty-four, Takejiro's business failed altogether, and he bought and now operated, with his son, a saké brewery. Within three years, Santoka was pressured into marrying a twenty-one-year-old woman, Sakino, and soon a son, Ken, was born. At first all went well, but soon his drinking problem turned for the worst.

In 1911, the well-known poet Seisensui launched the literary magazine *So'un* and Santoka offered this entry, for the first time abandoning his given name of Sho'ichi, and taking on his nom de plume:

My love's flesh
is bewitching;
summer butterflies.

Two years later, Santoka became a staff member of *So'un*, soon met Seisensui and was a key figure in the haiku community of Hofu.

Just after Santoka had become an editor at *So'un* in 1916, the saké brewery went bankrupt, his father fled under the cover of night and, with the help of friends, Santoka and his family ran off to the southern city of Kumamoto, and opened up a used-book store, the Garakuta. Within the next three years, his younger brother committed suicide, his grandmother passed away and his father died. Just before his father's passing, Santoka left Kumamoto for Tokyo and divorced Sakino, who would take care of him from time to time for the rest of his life. He wrote:

The last insect
left alive
circles the lamp.

One day in 1924, a drunken Santoka had a Mexican stand-off with a trolley car near the Kumamoto city hall. The trolley screeched to a halt, a crowd gathered, someone called the police, but a man suddenly stepped through the crowd and whisked Santoka away to a local Zen temple. There he stayed, took the Buddhist vows and was eventually given his own small temple, the Mitori Kannon, just outside of Kumamoto, to care for. Unable to sit still, however, within a year Santoka left to wander on "endless journeys."

Santoka's restlessness was displayed in all aspects of his life. Unable to live as a responsible husband, he left both wife and child; becoming a Buddhist priest in charge of a small temple and congregation, he ran away with nothing but two small rattan suitcases. On his perpetual wanderings, he sometimes slept out in the open or took brief lodging with friends. Small hermitages provided by admirers and disciples were also abandoned after a time. And there were times when neighbors or the police would have to take him home when he was found hopelessly drunk.

> The Milky Way at midnight;
> the drunkard?
> He dances.

Santoka happily admitted that he was incapable of anything other than writing haiku and wandering on his own two feet. Wandering, writing verses, and a love of sake were his karma, he said, and he lived out that karma to the very end. He finally passed away at the age of fifty-nine in his hermitage, the Isso-an, while a poetry reading was being conducted in the next room.

❦   ❦   ❦

Santoka wrote in the "free verse" style of Seisensui and Hosai, both of whom he greatly admired. Like them, he mostly ignored the 5-7-5 syllable standard and the season word, his haiku ranging anywhere from eight to twenty-four syllables. He was also influenced by the poet Seigetsu, and went to Ina twice to visit Seigetsu's grave, only to get caught in the snow and contract pneumonia the first time, but being successful the second. He also twice visited Hosai's grave on the island of Shodoshima.

Santoka wandered on his "endless journeys" for nearly twenty years, traveling as far as Hiraizumi in the north, down twice through the Kiso Road on his way south, and walking the eighty-eight temple pilgrimage around the island of Shikoku at least once. His Zen Buddhist precepts and his failure to keep them were often reflected in his verses and essays, and as many times as he fell, he always picked himself up again. His haiku are also imbued with his love of nature, and his love of the taste of free-running water. Near the end of his life, he wrote:

> The sound of water
> is unending;
> this is the Buddha.

❧   ❧   ❧

Haiku by Santoka

> From the thicket
> into my pot:
> one bamboo shoot.

藪から鍋へ筍いつぽん
Yabu kara nabe e takenoko ippon

> Suddenly peeking out
> in the spring wind:
> a bagworm.

春風の蓑虫ひょいとのぞいた
Harukaze no minomushi hyoi to nozoita

> Dressed in rags,
> layer on layer, the happy face
> of a simpleton.[1]

ぼろ着て着ぶれておめでたい顔で
Borokite kiburete omedetai kao de

---

1. *Omedetai* can be understood to mean both "happy" and "half-wit."

The temple bell,
    struck at dawn, struck at dusk;
  the pine wind.

松風に明け暮れの鐘ついて
Matsukaze ni akekure no kane tsuite

Soaked to the skin!
    Here's the stone guidepost
  showing the way.

しとどに濡れてこれは道しるべの石
Shitodo ni nurete kore wa michishirube no ishi

Walking around begging for alms.
    My gift:
  the scorching sun.

炎天をいただいて乞い歩く
Enten wo itadaite koiaruku

Giving a lift
    to the dragonfly;
  my bamboo hat.

笠にとんぼをとまらせてあるく
Kasa ni tonbo wo tomarasete aruku

Pleasantly drunk,
    falling
      leaves.

ほろほろ酔うて木の葉ふる
Horohoro youte ko no ha furu

Scratching
    the body, the fleas
left alive.

生き残つたからだ掻いている
Ikinokotta karada kaite iru

My bamboo hat
    is leaking,
too?

笠も濡れだしたか
Kasa mo nuredashita ka

Seen from behind
    as I go, my back
drenched in the autumn rain?

うしろすがたのしぐれてゆくか
Ushiro sugata no shigurete yuku ka

Right into
    my begging bowl:
hailstones.

鉄鉢の中へあられ
Teppachi no naka e arare

Until the very end,
    we travel and
clip our nails.

いつまで旅することの爪をきる
Itsu made tabi suru koto no tsume wo kiru

Pulling them out, pulling them out,
    and yet, pulling them out;
    the tenacity of weeds.

ぬいてもぬいても草の執着をぬく
Nuite mo nuite mo kusa no shuchaku wo nuku

Will the dragonfly alight,
    and me
    stark naked?

すっぱだかへとんぼとまろうとするか
Suppadaka e tonbo tomarou to suru ka

Today again,
    all day long, walking
    around in the wind.

けふもいちにら風をあるいてきた
Kyo mo ichinichi kaze wo aruite kita

Rain-soaked,
    on this willful, wayward journey,
    traveling on.

わがままきままな旅の雨にはぬれていく
Waga mama ki mama na tabi no ame ni wa nurete yuku

Moist with the morning dew,
    I go the way
    I want.

朝露しっとり行きたい方へ行く
Asatsuyu shittori ikitai hou e iku

Taking off my bamboo hat,
soaked through
and through.

笠をぬぎしみじみとぬれ
Kasa wo nugi shimijimi to nure

Always barking, one after another;
there's no other way
with dogs.

いつもつながれてほえるほかない犬です
Itsu mo tsunagarete hoeru hoka nai inu desu

The private parts of men and women, too;
the overflowing water,
of the bath.

ちんぽこもおそそも湧いてあふれる湯
Chinpoko mo ososo mo waite afureru yu

Sitting in weeds
that have become
my autumn.

秋となつた雑草にすわる
Aki to natta zassou ni suwaru

OGIWARA SEISENSUI
(1884–1976)

OGIWARA SEISENSUI WAS BORN in Tokyo, with the given name Tokichi. His father was a general goods retailer, about whom very little is recorded. In middle school he began to drink and smoke, was generally rebellious and was finally expelled for publishing a student newspaper criticizing the school's educational methods. With this turn of events, he became more serious, quit his drinking and smoking, gained entrance to another middle school and began writing haiku.

He was accepted into Tokyo Imperial University, studied linguistics and eventually entered Tokyo's haiku community, following Hekigodo's "New Haiku" movement (see page 131). In 1911, Seisensui and Hekigodo cofounded the literary magazine *So'un*, advocating the newest changes in the structure of haiku, which meant dropping the traditional 5-7-5 syllable count and the season word. Six years later, he was to split with Hekigodo, suggesting that haiku should be made into "free verse."

> A single bridge;
>> a child crosses, a dog crosses:
> morning.

In 1923, Seisensui lost his wife and daughter in the Great Kanto Earthquake, after which he took up residence at a chapel in the compound of the Buddhist temple Tofukuji in Kyoto. In the same year, he published *Tabibito Basho* [The traveler Basho], followed by a sequel of the same name in 1925. This then was followed by *Basho o tazunete* [Asking about Basho] in 1934.

During this period, Seisensui traveled extensively, always wearing a dyed-black priest's robe, carrying a single staff and umbrella and happily stopping at hot springs. But, like another traveler, Hekigodo, he was also happy to be home.

> Returning to my house,
>   and there I have
> my own bowl.

Although not ordained, he had a strong affinity for Buddhism, perhaps due to the loss of siblings as a child and then the deaths of his family as an adult. He wrote,

> Dimly, the chant,
>   Praise to the Buddha Shakyamuni;
> tinted maple leaves

and,

> I believe in the Buddha
>   and the Truth
> and the green of barley.[1]

Seisensui remarried in 1929 and moved with his wife to Kamakura. He then moved back to Tokyo, but his house was destroyed during Second World War bombing raids, and in 1944 he returned to Kamakura where he would continue to live for the rest of his life.

---

1. Compare this with a haiku-ized rendering of H. D. Thoreau:
> I believe in the forest,
>   and in the meadow,
> and in the night in which the corn grows.

❧   ❧   ❧

Seisensui was a popular teacher of haiku. His students included Santoka and Hosai, whose works he originally published in *So'un*. He was not immune to new technologies, and went on national radio delivering lectures on haiku and literary criticism. His more than two hundred works include *Seisensui kushu* [Seisensui's collected verse], *Haiku teisho* [Talks on haiku] and a number of travelogues. His haiku tended to be simple and homely, and he seems to have had a special affection for sparrows.

> The sparrows, mother and child,
>   and I
> at this one day's end.

❧   ❧   ❧

Haiku by Seisensui

> How lonely!
>   This whole day,
> not one wonderful thing.

さびしや此の一日一つの不思議をも見ざりし
Sabishi ya kono ichinichi hitotsu no fushigi wo mo mizarishi

> Throughout the year, the same thing:
>   at the desk since dawn,
> the sky that has become spring.

年中同じものが机にけさから春になった空
Nenchuu onaji mono ga tsukue ni kesa kara haru ni natta sora

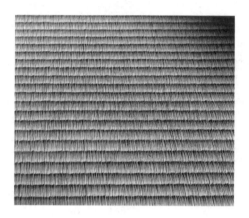

Bring some mushrooms from out back;
  on the tatami,
    rays of sun.

裏から茸とつて来て日のさしている畳
Ura kara take totte kite hi no sashite iru tatami

The skylark,
    sings in the sky, sings on earth,
  sings, flying away.

雲雀天上で鳴き大地で鳴き鳴きながら上り
Hibari tenjou de naki daichi de naki nakinagara nobori

Snow falls
　　　into the stream, falls
　　from inside the stream.

雪水に降る水の中から降る
Yuki mizu ni furu mizu no naka kara furu

A winter night
　　　with my own shadow,
　　writing about myself.

冬の夜のおのが影とおのが事書く
Fuyu no yo no ono ga kage to ono ga koto kaku

People going along,
　　　getting as wet
　　as the wet buds on the trees.

木の芽ぬれるはどは人のぬれて行く
Ki no me nureru hodo wa hito no nurete yuku

When cicadas cry, they cry,
　　　the cicadas cry together,
　　the day coming to an end.

蜩鳴けば鳴けば蜩鳴きつれ日ぐるる
Higurashi nakeba nakeba higurashi nakitsure higururu

In place of the straw hat
　　　hung on the wall, tied up
　　tea flowers.

笠は掛けるところにかかり茶の花
Kasa wa kakeru tokoro ni kakari cha no hana

The person sending me off and his shadow,
I, being sent off and my shadow;
frogs on a moonlit night.

送る人と影と送られる私の影も月夜の蛙
Okuru hito to kage to okurareru watakushi
no kage mo tsukiyo no kawazu

Going outside, nice and warm;
in my pocket, a book
the color of dry grass.

いでてあたたかし枯草いろの本をふところ
Idete atatakashi karekusa iro no hon wo futokoro

The sky, a blue emptiness,
on the ground, white snow;
sparrows.

空は青空、地は白雪の雀です
Sora wa aozora, chi wa shirayuki no suzume desu

Completely naked,[2]
I write and offer up a thought
for today.

裸でけふの感想一つ書きあげました
Hadaka de kyou no kansou hitotsu kakiagemashita

---

2. *Hadaka* can mean either naked or penniless. To my knowledge, Seisensui
was never poor.

The sparrows, mother and child,
    and I
  at this one day's end.

雀の親と子とわたくしのいちにち暮れてゐる

Suzume no oya to ko to watakushi no ichinichi kurete iru

Autumn rains;
      today I sit with my own
  simple meal.

秋雨、けふは自分のうちの茶漬に座り

Akisame, kyou wa jibun no uchi no chazuke ni suwari

Lighting a fire in the brazier,
      returning from my journey;
  falling rain.

火鉢に火を入れ旅をもどると雨のふり

Hibachi ni hi wo ire tabi wo modoru to ame no furi

In this rain, the rain
      melting the snow, the sparrows
  are getting wet.

この雨で雪の消える雨に雀がぬれてゐる

Kono ame de yuki no kieru ame ni suzume ga nurete iru

Waiting for the trolley,
      at my feet, a butterfly;
  already summer.

電車を待つと足もとてふてふがもう夏

Densha wo matsu to ashimoto chocho ga mou natsu

Still some evening light,
  now the glitter of a firefly
in the child's hand.

まだ夕明りの、もう光る蛍が児の手に
Mada yuuakari no, mou hikaru hotaru ga ko no te ni

Reflected in the wash basin:
  the leaves of the plum,
the fruit of the plum.

洗面にうつるのが梅の葉の梅の実
Senmen ni utsuru no ga ume no ha no ume no mi

The moon this bright night has gone,
  the waves have gone, too;
a small saké cup.

月夜の月もない波もない小さかづき
Tsukiyo no tsuki mo nai nami mo nai shosakazuki

Snow falling, falling; the radio
  informing us of our troops, and again
informing us of our troops.[3]

雪はふるふるラジオは兵に告ぐ又兵に告ぐ
Yuki wa furu furu rajio ha hei ni tsugu mata hei ni tsugu

---

3. Written in1937, during the Second Sino-Japanese war

OZAKI HOSAI
(1885–1926)

OZAKI HOSAI WAS BORN Ozaki Hideo in what is now the city of Tottori in Tottori Prefecture. His father was a secretary at the Tottori courthouse. Hosai had an early interest in haiku and was composing poems from the age of fourteen. He felt, however, that poetry would not lead to a settled career and so he enrolled at the law school at Tokyo Imperial University. At about the age of twenty-one or twenty-two, he proposed marriage to a young lady, but this was rejected by his intended's older brother. By the time he graduated from law school, he had developed a serious drinking problem, had changed his given name to Hosai (放哉, "Letting Go") and had fallen into alcohol abuse.

Employed as a lawyer by an insurance company, Hosai was well liked at work and steadily promoted. He married a nineteen-year-old girl about whom little is known other than her name, Kaoru. Hosai's alcoholism worsened, however, and he was eventually let go by his employer. Finding work with another insurance company in Seoul, Korea, he moved to that country, but came down with what was diagnosed as pleurisy, and returned to Japan.

Hosai then spent several years either in sanatoriums or employed as a temple sexton at various temples, often losing even that work because of his drinking. At age forty, with the help of his friend the poet Seisensui, he was given permission to reside in the Nango-an, a small hermitage attached to the Saikoji temple on the island of Shodoshima. During the final years of his life, he associated with Seisensui and the fishermen of Shodoshima and their families. He also continued to write haiku, which were published in the literary magazines *So'un* and *Hototogisu*.

Hosai's health diminished in 1925, with recurring bouts of pleurisy. Seisensui and other friends in haiku had him taken care of by a local fisherman's wife, but he died on April 7, 1926.

❧   ❧   ❧

Hosai adhered to the new "free verse" haiku advocated by Heki-godo, Seisensui, Santoka and others, disregarding the traditional 5-7-5 syllable format and often leaving out a season word. He wrote about his poverty and loneliness, his devotion to Buddhism and his attraction to women.

> The road
>   of myself alone,
> coming to an end.

> Wiping off the morning desk.
>   with a great voice,
> the Buddhist sutras.

> Her breasts like upside down lacquered bowls;
>   white clouds rising,
> plump and firm.

At the end of his essay, "Shima ni kuru made" [Coming to the island], Hosai quotes the confessional from the Kannon Sutra:

> All the bad karma I have created since times long passed
> Are due to my beginningless greed, anger and stupidity.
> These have been born from my body, speech and mind,
>   and I now repent all of them.[1]

---

1. Ikeuchi Osamu, ed. *Ozaki hosai kushu*. Tokyo: Iwanami shoten, 2015.

✤   ✤   ✤

Haiku by Hosai

Tea flowers;
    rustling about my hermitage,
winter sparrows.

茶の花や庵さざめかず寒雀
Cha no hana ya iori sazamekazu kansuzume

Asleep, I heard it:
    a mosquito
singing of long, long ago.

寝て聞けば遠き昔を鳴く蚊かな
Nete kikeba tooki mukashi wo naku ka kana

Drawing out the soul
    of the prostitute;
an afternoon nap.

傾城の魂ぬけし昼寝かな
Keisei no tama nukeshi hirune kana

All my old socks:
    just one
of each pair.

古足袋のみんな片足ばかり
Furutabi no minna kataashi bakari

Returning along the beach,
   all my footprints
      gone.

なぎさふりかへる我が足跡も無く
Nagisa furikaeru waga ashiato mo naku

This morning at my hermitage
   they were early!
      Sparrows.

今朝は庵が早かつたぞ雀
Kesa wa iori ga hayakatta zo suzume

Given time off
   by the Buddha,
      I do the laundry.

仏にひまをもらつて洗濯してゐる
Hotoke ni hima wo moratte sentaku shite iru

The beggar woman,
what big
breasts!

女乞食の大きな乳房かな
Onna kojiki no ookina chibusa kana

The bug playing dead
got up
and walked out.

死んだ真似した虫が歩き出した
Shinda mane shita mushi ga arukidashita

Holding my hands
over a hibachi
without a flame.

火の無い火鉢に手をかざす
Hi no nai hibachi ni te wo kazasu

The flies
have taken a liking
to my bald head.

禿げあたまを蠅に好かれて居る
Hageatama wo hae ni sukarete iru

Wiping off the morning desk,
with a great voice,
the Buddhist sutras.

朝の机ふくやひやひや経文
Asa no tsukue fuku ya hiyahiya kyoumon

My skinny buttocks
stabbed
by the cushion.

痩せた尻が座布団に突きささる
Yaseta shiri ga zabuton ni tsukisasaru

Silent all morning,
the mosquito
came in and bit me.

だまりこんで居る朝から蚊がさしに来た
Damarikonde iru asa kara ka ga sashi ni kita

Stole in and bit me, then
sneaked out:
the mosquito.

こつそり蚊が刺して行つたひつそり
Kossori ka ga sashite itta hissori

Having sucked enough blood,
the mosquito
fell over and died.

血を吸ひ足つた蚊がころりと死んでしまつた
Chi wo suitatta ka ga korori to shinde shimatta

Proud of her songs,
the old lady
is hoping for saké.

うたが自慢でおばば酒をほしがる
Uta ga jiman de o-baba sake wo hoshigaru

In the moist air
she lets her breasts
hover in the evening breeze.

汐ふくむ夕風に乳房垂れたり
Shio fukumu yuukaze ni chibusa taretari

Husband and wife
sneezing
and laughing.

夫婦でくしゃめして笑った
Fuufu de kushame shite waratta

Her breasts like upside down lacquered bowls
white clouds rising,
plump and firm.

お椀を伏せたやうな乳房むくむくもりあがるしらくも
O-wan wo fuseta you na chibusa mukumuku moriagaru shirakumo

Having had my say,
I walked out of the gate;
a drizzling shower.

申し置いて門を出れば時雨哉
Moshioite kado wo dereba shigure kana

The road
of myself, alone,
coming to an end.

一人の道が暮れて来た
Hitori no michi ga kurete kita

SUGITA HISAJO
(1890–1946)

SUGITA HISAJO WAS BORN in what is now Kagoshima City, the third daughter of the secretary of the Finance Minister. As her father, Akahori Renzo, was transferred from post to post, the family moved to Okinawa; Taipei; and finally Kokura in Kyushu. She has said that her first memories are of the ocean.

Hisajo married a painter and teacher of the fine arts, Sugita Udai, a dream marriage for her. In 1911, she gave birth to a daughter, Masako, who later became a haiku poet. In 1916, a second daughter was born; and Hisajo's older brother, Akahori Gessen, who was a haiku poet, took lodging at her house and taught her the techniques of haiku. Until that time, she had wanted to become a novelist, but now began writing haiku in earnest, submitting her verses to the haiku magazine *Hototogisu*, where they appeared the following year.

In 1917, Hisajo met Takahama Kyoshi at a haiku gathering and immediately took him as a teacher. In the meantime, to her disappointment, her husband had stopped painting.

> Darning socks;
>   I am not a "modern" free woman,
>   but the wife of a teacher.

Her home life deteriorated, and she became more obsessed with Kyoshi, her admiration for him becoming publicly apparent.

In 1932, she supervised the publication of an all-women's haiku magazine, *Hanakoromo*, but it did not survive its fifth issue. Two years later, she became a staff member of *Hototogisu* magazine. As her fascination with Kyoshi became more intense, she wrote to him three times asking him to write an introduction to a collection of her haiku, yet her requests were ignored and the book was not published. Desperate to meet him, she traveled to Tokyo, but was rebuffed again. In 1936, her name was dropped from *Hototogisu*, a shock which resulted in depression and physical weakening. Finally, in 1939, she compiled a manuscript of all her verses that summarized her life as a haiku poet.

Hisajo had suffered from kidney disease earlier on in her life, and now, in October of 1945, she suffered from malnutrition due to wartime food shortages, and was hospitalized. On January 1 of the following year, she passed away in the hospital due to complications of kidney disease, and was said to have died insane. She was initially buried in the Sugita family grave in Toyota City, but eventually her remains were divided and part of them buried in the Akahori gravesite in Matsumoto.

Hisajo had a strong influence on the women poets who were to follow her, but her outspokenness and unrestrained conduct tarnished her reputation. In 1952, her daughter Masako finally published *Sugita Hisajo kushu* [A haiku collection of Sugita Hisajo] and her genius was recognized.

Haiku by Hisajo

Shelling chestnuts;
    how happy the children in beddy-bye will be
tomorrow.

栗むくやたのしみ寝ねし子らの明日
Kuri muku ya tanoshimi neneshi kora no asu

Flowing in the spring tide,
      duckweed,
    as swift as an arrow.

春潮に流るる藻あり矢の如く
Shunchou ni nagaruru mo ari ya no gotoku

Plum-blossom viewing;
    running around
    in travel clothes.

探梅に走り参じたる旅衣
Tanbai ni hashiri sanjitaru tabigoromo

Fishing boats lined up
    in front of the tower;
    the evening cool.[1]

晩涼や釣舟並ぶ楼の前
Banryou ya tsuribune narabu rou no mae

---

1. The tower is likely a lookout structure for the fishing vessels.

Darning socks;
   I am not a "modern" free woman,
   but the wife of a teacher.

足袋つぐやノラともならず教師妻

Tabi tsugu ya nora to mo narazu kyoshizuma

An echo; the mountain cuckoo,
      wayward
      and self-willed.

谺して山ほととぎすほしいまま

Kodama shite yama hototogisu hoshiimama

Field cranes dancing,
      the circle of the sun
      rising over the peaks.

田鶴舞ふや日輪峰を登りくる

Tazuru mau ya nichirin mine wo noborikuru

Pausing at the evening glories
after washing
and scrubbing.

夕顔に水仕もすみてたたずめり
Yuugao ni mizushi mo sumite tatazumeri

On the great peak
the call of a crane echoes
and ends.

大嶺にこだます鶴の声すめり
Oomine ni kodama su tsuru no koe sumeri

Gently falling asleep,
the happiness of a comforter;
an autumn night.

ふわと寝て蒲団嬉しき秋夜かな
Fuwa to nete futon ureshiki aki-yo kana

In the dark great waves
of the black sea,
a wild goose calls.

玄海のおおなみのくらさや雁叫ぶ
Genkai no oonami no kurasa ya gan sakebu

On the great peak,
I walked on and on,
looking at autumn leaves.

大嶺に歩み迫りぬ紅葉狩
Oomine ni ayumi semarinu momijigari

Calling in at our mountain home,
　　it was dark;
　　first winter rains.

訪れて山家は暗し初時雨
Otozurete sanke wa kurashi hatsu shigure

Looking in on the flowers
　　at our thatched home
　　in my old home town.

古里の藁屋の花をたづねけり
Furusato no waraya no hana wo tazunekeri

An eastern wind blows
　　my hair from around my neck,
　　showing my ears.

東風吹くや耳現はるるうなゐ髪
Kochi fuku ya mimi arawaruru unaigami

Folding paper handkerchiefs
　　for the new schoolchild,
　　and sending her off.

入学児に鼻紙折りて持たせけり
Nyugakuji ni hanagami orite motasekeri

Loneliness in the midst
　　of a bewildering
　　spring night.

春の夜のまどゐの中にゐて寂し
Haru no yo no madoi no naka ni ite sabishi

Autumn has come,
I buy small mackerel
the color of sapphires.

秋来ぬとサファイア色の小鯵買う
Aki kinu to safaia iro no koaji kau

Far away,
a clear winter sky;
cranes dancing.

冬晴の雲井はるかに田鶴まへる
Fuyubare no kumoi haruka ni tazuru maeru

Above the high peak,
a star is visible;
pleasant climbing tomorrow.

高嶺星見出てうれし明日登山
Takaneboshi midete ureshi ashita tozan

My upbringing:
swimming in a blue sea
in perpetual summer.

常夏の碧き潮あびわがそだつ
Tokonatsu no aoki shio'abi waga sodatsu

Like a plank of wood
stuck in my sash:
the autumn fan.

板の如き帯にさされぬ秋扇
Ita no gotoki obi ni sasarenu aki oogi

LESS WELL-KNOWN HAIKU POETS

MATSUNAGA TEITOKU (1571–1653)

NOZAWA BONCHO (1640–1714)

MUKAI KYORAI (1651–1704)

OCHI ETSUJIN (1656–1730)

TAKARAI KIKAKU (1661–1707)

FUKUDA CHIYO-NI (1703–1775)

HASHIMOTO TAKAKO (1899–1963)

MITSUHASHI TAKAJO (1899–1972)

NAKAMURA TEIJO (1900–1988)

HOSHINO TATSUKO (1903–1984)

MATSUNAGA TEITOKU
(1571–1653)

MATSUNAGA TEITOKU WAS BORN in Kyoto into a samurai family. Teitoku's father was a professional linked-verse poet, his mother was the sister of the well-known Neo-Confucian philosopher Fujiwara Seika, and his grandfather was a high-ranking general.

Teitoku is described as having been a *bunjin* (文人), a member of the literati. The Japanese term implies not only interest in the literary, but in other arts as well, including the martial arts. When Teitoku was young, he associated with the scholars and artists of the day, including feudal lord and poet Hosokawa Yusai, from whom he learned classical *waka* poetry and linked verse. Another of Teitoku's acquaintances, the Neo-Confucian scholar Hayashi Razan, encouraged him to begin giving public lectures in the Japanese classics, and in 1620 he opened the Teitoku School, first educating the children of the common people and later tutoring poets.

An extremely prolific poet, Teitoku wrote both haiku and *kyoka* or "crazy poems." He dealt with lighter subjects, expressing more interest in the material than in the spiritual, but was not so irreverent that he went against the Confucian and Buddhist morality of the day:

> The bush warbler and the frog
> have no need
> of a teacher of poetry.

Among Teitoku's many disciples was Kigin, Basho's teacher of haiku, who was famous for the haiku,

> The shape
> of the autumn wind:
> clumps of miscanthus.

Teitoku died at the age of eighty-three. His death poem was not a haiku, but rather a waka:

> "Tomorrow will be just like this,"
> we think the day before.
> But today we realize
> that all is change:
> This is the way of the world.

❦   ❦   ❦

Haiku by Teitoku

> A rustic temple
> in bad repair, but in the ruins,
> the shining platform of the Buddha.

野寺あれて跡にやはゆる仏の座
Nodera arete ato ni ya hayuru hotoke no za

> On the hip of the mountain
> wearing a sash of clouds;
> an evening shower.

山の腰にはく夕立や雲の帯
Yama no koshi ni haku yuudachi ya kumo no obi

Stars on a hot night;
    are they heat rash?
The broad sky.

暑き夜の星はあせぼかあまの原
Atsuki yo no hoshi wa asebo ka ama no hara

The seed for everyone
    taking a midday nap:
the autumn moon.

皆人の昼寝の種や秋の月
Mina hito no hirune no tane ya aki no tsuki

Indoors for the winter;
    even the crickets
have their wise burrows.

冬籠り虫けらまでも穴かしこ
Fuyugomori mushikera made mo ana kashiko

Amusingly
    the leaves on the tree fall
by ones and twos.

おもしろくはらはら落る木葉哉
Omoshiroku hara hara ochiru ko no ha kana

The cloud: a snake
    eating up the frog
of the moon.

雲は蛇呑みこむ月のかえるかな
Kumo wa hebi nomikomu tsuki no kaeru kana

Can Mount Fuji alone
    become snow covered
in just one night?

富士のみか一夜にでくる雪の山
Fuji nomi ka hitoyo ni dekuru yuki no yama

It emerged perfectly round;
    but how long it is,
the spring day.

まんまるいづれどながき春日かな
Manmaru izuredo nagaki haruhi kana

Staring at the knots
    in the pillow;
the long night.

くくり目を見つつ夜長き枕かな
Kukurime wo mitsutsu yo nagaki makura kana

181

NOZAWA BONCHO
(1640–1714)

NOZAWA BONCHO WAS BORN in Kanazawa but little is known of his background other than that his family name was either Nozawa or Miyagi. He was practicing medicine in Kyoto when he met Basho and became one of his most devoted disciples. In 1690, he edited *Saru mino* [The monkey's raincoat], with Kyorai, another of Basho's disciples. This work was an anthology of the work of the Basho school of poets, in which Boncho included over forty of his own verses. Not long after, he became estranged from Basho and moved to Osaka.

In 1693, Boncho became involved with some secret dealings with Dutch traders, was arrested and served a prison term of five years. Upon release, he continued to write haiku, but of lower quality, and lived in poverty.

Boncho's haiku was known for its clarity of description and for its delicate treatment of natural scenery.

> Throughout the town,
>   the smells of this and that,
>   under a summer moon.

> The brushwood,
>   though already cut,
>   is beginning to bud.

Boncho's wife, Ukou, also a haiku poet of some renown, took care of Basho when he was staying at Kyorai's hermitage. Various biographers have recounted the story of a cold, snowy night when Boncho, along with a twelve-year-old servant, was on his way out of the house to attend a poetry party. Before he could close the door, Ukou came up with this poem,

> Were he my child,
>   I would not bring him along;
> a night of snow.

Boncho was abashed and went to the party leaving the servant at home.

❧　　❧　　❧

Haiku by Boncho

> All piled up!
>   A mountain with snow
> is just a mountain.

かさなるや雪のある山只の山
Kasanaru ya yuki no aru yama tada no yama

> I called back the carp seller,
>   but he couldn't be seen
> in the hail.

呼かへす鮒売見えぬあられ哉
Yobikaesu funauri mienu arare kana

The razor
　　　rusted in a single night;
　　early summer rain.

髪剃や一夜に錆びて五月雨
Kamisori ya hito yo ni sabite samidare

Three leaves fall,
　　　leaving a withered tree;
　　the paulownia sapling.

三葉ちりて跡はかれ木や桐の苗
Mitsuba chirite ato wa kareki ya kiri no nae

Crossing the stream,
　　　gazing at flowers
　　of duckweed.

渡り懸けて藻の花のぞく流哉
Watarikakete mo no hana nozoku nagare kana

Companion to the blowing wind;
in the sky,
a single moon.

吹く風の相手や空に月一つ
Fuku kaze no aite ya sora ni tsuki hitotsu

Throughout the city,
the smells of this and that
under a summer moon.

市中は物の匂ひや夏の月
Ichi naka wa mono no nioi ya natsu no tsuki

Behind the line of granaries,
the back and forth path
of swallows.

蔵並ぶ裏は燕のかよひ道
Kura narabu ura wa tsubame no kayoi michi

What kind of wretch
would pee here
on this first snow?

初雪にこの小便は何やつぞ
Hatsu yuki ni kono shouben wa nani yatsu zo

Even without the wind,
the falling leaves
of the paulowania.

桐の木の風にかまはぬ落葉かな
Kiri no ki no kaze ni kamawanu ochiba kana

MUKAI KYORAI

(1651–1704)

MUKAI KYORAI WAS BORN in Hizen, the current Nagasaki Prefecture, on the southern island of Kyushu, but moved to Kyoto when he was seven. His father was a Confucian scholar and a physician, but the boy was brought up mostly by his mother. As a young man, Kyorai returned to Kyushu, excelled in archery and other martial arts and was offered a position in the Fukuoka fiefdom. He declined the offer, however and went back to Kyoto where he assisted his older brother, who was now a court physician. At the age of twenty-five, he gave up the martial arts altogether.

In 1686, Kyorai went to Edo (modern-day Tokyo) and made friends with the haiku poet Kikaku, who introduced him to Matsuo Basho. Kyorai became devoted to Basho and three years later, the famous haiku poet stayed at Kyorai's hermitage in Saga to write his *Saga nikki* [Saga diary]. This place later became famous as the *rakujisha*, or "the hut of falling persimmons," as a storm knocked off all the fruit from his trees the very night Kyorai had promised to sell them to someone. He wrote,

> The master of the persimmons;
> the branches close by,
> a mountain storm.

On the wall of the hermitage were written precepts encouraging those who read them to enjoy *haikai* (haiku) while staying there, to not speak of the world's quibbling and to think with strict concentration day and night.

In 1691, Basho enlisted Kyorai and Nozawa Boncho to edit *Saru mino* [The monkey's raincoat], an anthology of the work of the Basho school of poets, after which Boncho and Basho parted ways. Kyorai, on the other hand, became known as one of the "ten disciples" of Basho. He would later write the book the *Kyoraisho* [Kyorai's writings], providing anecdotes of Basho's life and the poet's theories of haiku and linked verse. One of the more interesting of these theories is that of *nioi-zuke* (匂付), link by scent: that one verse carries the atmosphere of its predecessor much as the fragrance of a flower is carried by the wind. The *Kyoraisho* is considered to be an important literary document even today.

Kyorai's brothers, sister and wife were also haiku poets of some note. He himself was said to be a warm and gentle person, personality traits that were reflected in his verses.

> How sad;
>   the firefly's light goes out
> in my hand.

> On a night like this,
>   I gazed at the moon; sending them off
> at the crematory.

When Basho lay dying in 1694, it was Kyorai and Kikaku who took care of him to the end.

Haiku by Kyorai

Early spring!
    I'll put on the sword
  bequeathed to my family.

初春や家に譲りの太刀はかん
Hatsu haru ya ie ni yuzuri no tachi hakan

Though he moves,
    I cannot see clearly, the man
  working the field.

うごくとも見えで畑うつ男かな
Ugoku tomo miede hatake utsu otoko kana

It moves along slipping,
    doing its best, the frog
  on the river bank.

いくすべり骨おる岸のかはづ哉
Iku suberi hone oru kishi no kawazu kana

They must be busy!
  Out in the offing, early winter rain;
full sails, reefed sails.

いそがしや沖の時雨の真帆片帆
Isogashi ya oki no shigure no maho kataho

No certainty at all
      about head or tail;
   the sea slug.

尾頭のこころもとなき海鼠哉

Okashira no kokoromoto naki namako kana

The rough seashore;
      used to running and dashing,
   a flock of plovers.

あら磯やはしり馴れたる友衛

Ara'iso ya hashirinareta tomochidori

On a rice-field footpath
    now croaking, now silent;
  the frogs.

一畔はしばし啼きやむ蛙かな

Hito aze wa shibashi naki yamu kawazu kana

In the dawn
    it's difficult to turn over;
  the cold!

有明にふりむきがたき寒さ哉

Ariake ni furimukigataki samusa kana

Sadly going out
    in my hand;
  the lightning bug.

手の上に悲しく消ゆる蛍かな

Te no ue ni kanashiku kiyuru hotaru kana

In the back of the shelf,
    my parents' mortuary tablets;
  their dear old faces.

玉棚の奥なつかしや親の顔

Tamadana no oku natsukashi ya oya no kao

Nights when the mendicants
    do not beat their begging bowls
  lack clarity.

鉢叩来ぬ夜となれば朧なり

Hachitataki konu yo to nareba oboro nari

OCHI ETSUJIN
(1656–1730)

OCHI ETSUJIN WAS BORN in northern Echigo, now Niigata Prefecture. Eventually he left and moved to Nagoya, where he met Basho and became one of his disciples. He was said to be a high-minded and handsome man who enjoyed saké.

Etsujin immersed himself in the Chinese and Japanese classics, and his haiku style was often intellectual and based on ancient literature. An example of this might be

> The years passing by;
> I hide my gray hairs
> from my parents.

referring, perhaps, to the old Chinese custom of always acting childish in front of one's parents so they will not notice themselves getting old.

In his later years, Etsujin distanced himself from the Basho coterie, but his haiku stagnated and even after he returned to that community the quality of his verse remained poor. Still, he is counted as one of Basho's "ten disciples." Basho seemed to enjoy Etsujin's company, and the two went on a trip to Sarashina, now part of the city of Nagano, recounted in Basho's travel sketch *Sarashina Kiko* [A visit to Sarashina village]. It was on this trip that Etsujin fell off of his horse while drunk, moving Basho to write,

> Snow and sand;
> falling off a horse
> while drunk on saké.

Etsujin's motto was "two days of hard work, two days of play; three days of hard work, three days of play." When happily drunk, he would chant verses from the fourteenth-century martial epic, *The Tale of the Heike*. He is buried at the Choenji temple in Nagoya. His death verse is,

A late autumn evening;
shall I light a lamp?
she comes to ask.

❦   ❦   ❦

Haiku by Etsujin

Among
scattered flowers;
old folk tales.

散花の間はむかしばなしかな
Chiru hana no aida wa mukashibanashi kana

Though flowering,
I decided to replant it:
the peony.

花ながら植かへらるる牡丹かな
Hana nagara uekaeraruru botan kana

Morning
   seems difficult
for the croaking frog.

あかつきをむつかしさうに鳴蛙
Akatsuki wo mutsukashisou ni naku kawazu

Though I went so far
   as to break off and send the camellias;
the cherry blossoms!

つばきまで折そへらるるさくら哉
Tsubaki made ori soeraruru sakura kana

Peacefully, quietly,
I passed by
the willow.

何事もなしと過行柳哉
Nanigoto mo nashi to sugiyuku yanagi kana

The paper lamps have become sooty;
a cold night
of snow.

行灯の煤けて寒き雪のくれ
Andon no susukete samuki yuki no kure

After seeing
the first snow,
I washed my face.

初雪を見てから顔を洗ひけり
Hatsuyuki wo mite kara kao wo araikeri

When I gave up
and thought it inevitable;
cats in love.

羨やまし思ひきるとき猫の恋
Urayamashi omoikiru toki neko no koi

When I turned and checked,
the white plastered wall looked dirty
in the evening mist.

見かへれば白かべいやし夕がすみ
Mikaereba shirakabe iyashi yuugasumi

194

TAKARAI KIKAKU
(1661–1707)

TAKARAI KIKAKU WAS BORN in the new capital of Edo (modern-day Tokyo), the eldest son of well-to-do physician and haiku poet, Takenoshita Tojun. At first setting out to be a doctor, Kikaku received a full education not just in medicine, but in Confucianism, Japanese literature, Chinese poetry and painting. By the age of eighteen, he was recognized as a talented haiku poet and eventually became one of the "ten disciples" of Basho.

This was the beginning of the Genroku period (1688–1704), however, an era of expansive economics, a colorful urban culture and a general pursuit of pleasure, and Kikaku was happy to immerse himself in this milieu, passing his days in drinking and boisterous singing. It is said that he felt slightly scolded by Basho's poem,

> I am a man
> who eats his breakfast
> looking at morning glories,

but undeterred by this ideal of refined simplicity, he continued in his colorful expressions of city life of Edo:

> A dark night;
> the moon shines only
> on the gay quarters.

Vomiting at dawn,
      is that my neighbor
or a cuckoo?

Kikaku and Basho initially had a close master–disciple relationship, but this eventually developed into an ambivalent rivalry. To demonstrate his opposition to Basho's extreme aestheticism, the younger poet "corrected" the first line of the master's most famous poem, "An old pond / a frog jumps in / the sound of water" to "A mountain rose / a frog jumps in / the sound of water," creating an entirely different impression. Basho, in turn, sometimes criticized Kikaku's haiku as exaggerated or flippant. Regardless of Kikaku's differences with Basho, however, it was he and Kyorai who attended the great poet as he lay dying.

As an indication of his life as a "child of Edo," Kikaku was among the strong supporters of the famous forty-seven samurai who ignored the edict of the shogunate and took revenge on the daimyo lord whom they felt had caused their master's death. Very soon after the shogunate commanded that the forty-seven commit ritual suicide, puppet plays, essays and other genres appeared in sympathy with them. Kikaku continued with his prodigal lifestyle and saké drinking, which were said to be the cause of his death at the young age of forty-six.

Oddly, an India-ink painting of Kikaku depicts the poet as a rather portly, unhappy person holding a spray of flowers. Another painting, in color, shows the same very heavy man with a smile and holding what appears to be a pipe.

Haiku by Kikaku

Lightning!
      Yesterday in the east,
today in the west.

稲妻や昨日は東今日は西
Inazuma ya kinou wa higashi kyou wa nishi

A night of croaking frogs;
      so many stars
on the bay.

ここかしこ蛙鳴く江の星の数
Koko kashiko kawazu naku e no hoshi no kazu

The snow on my straw hat
      is lighter when I think
it is mine.

我雪と思へば軽し笠の上
Waga yuki to omoeba karoshi kasa no ue

Winter has come;
      alighting on the scarecrow,
a crow.

冬来ては案山子にとまる烏かな
Fuyu kite wa kakashi ni tomaru karasu kana

Ah, the beggar!
      He wears heaven and earth
for summer clothes.

乞食かな天地を着たる夏衣
Kojiki kana tenchi wo kitaru natsugoromo

The tree frog,
      riding the banana leaf
swaying in the wind.

雨蛙芭蕉にのりて戦ぎけり
Amagaeru bashou ni norite soyogikeri

In the light of the setting sun,
      flying throughout the town,
butterflies.

夕日影町中に飛ぶこてふかな
Yuuhi kage machinaka ni tobu kochou kana

An evening shower;
      coming round the house,
quacking ducks.

夕だちや家をめぐりて啼く家鴨
Yuudachi ya ie wo megurite naku ahiru

The evening cool;
      fortunate indeed
  to be born a man.

夕涼みよくぞ男に生れけり
Yuusuzumi yoku zo otoko ni umarekeri

This garden gate
      chained up tight;
  the winter moon.

この木戸や鎖の刺されて冬の月
Kono kido ya kusari no sasarete fuyu no tsuki

FUKUDA CHIYO-NI
(1703–1775)

FUKUDA CHIYO-NI, also known as Kaga no Chiyo or Kaga no Chiyojo, was born in Matto Village, Kaga Province (now Ishikawa Prefecture) near the Japan Sea. She was the eldest daughter of a scroll mounter, but despite her commoner origin, she began writing haiku at an early age. At the age of twelve, she began studying under a haiku master who had studied under Basho.

At age seventeen, she met the haiku poet Shiko,[1] who was then on a walking journey through Japan. She invited him to her home and asked to become his disciple. Shiko said, "Well then, write a haiku," and gave her the subject of a cuckoo. She thought throughout the night and the next day presented this poem:

> "Cuckoo!"
> Then again, "Cuckoo!" I called,
> but dawn had come.

This was highly praised by Shiko, who recognized her talent, and after this, her name became recognized throughout Japan.

Chiyo-ni is said to have married at eighteen to a lower-ranked samurai, Fukuoka Yahachi, who died but two years later. Other reports declare that she was never married at all. At any rate, by her early twenties she was living with her elderly parents in Matto, and carried on with their scroll-mounting business. After

---

1. Shiko was early on a Zen monk, but later practiced medicine. He established his own school of haiku and was a prolific writer. If he was on a walking tour in her area, she surely would have heard about it.

they died, she eventually adopted a married couple to take over the business.

In her fifties, Chiyo-ni cut her hair, became a Buddhist nun and took the name Soen. She continued writing haiku, leaving over 1,700 verses, and at age seventy-two wrote an introduction to Yosa Buson's *Tamamoshu* [Collection of seaweed], an anthology of women poets of the seventeenth and eighteenth centuries, published in 1774.

Chiyo-ni passed away at seventy-three and is buried at the Seikoji temple. Her death verse was,

> Looking at the moon,
> how amusing,
> this world.

Much of Chiyo-ni's poetry concerns nature and living a simple life of observation, as in the following:

> Spring rain!
> All and everything
> becomes beautiful.

The verse for which she is best known is:

> The well-bucket,
> taken by the morning glory;
> I borrow water.

Haiku by Chiyo-ni

Plum flowers blooming;
    no matter if it rains or snows
  spring is spring.

梅さくや何がふっても春は春
Ume saku ya nani ga futte mo haru wa haru

The nightingale;
    rephrasing itself,
    rephrasing itself again.

鶯やまた言ひなほし言ひなほし
Uguisu ya mata iinaoshi iinaoshi

Departing autumn;
    caressing my single life,
  the sound of the pines.

ゆく秋やひとり身をもむ松のこゑ
Yuku aki ya hitori mi wo momu matsu no koe

Crouching down,
    watching the clouds;
  the frog.

踞ばうて雲をうかがふ蛙かな
Tsukubaute kumo wo ukagau kawazu kana

If it had no voice,
    we would miss the heron altogether;
  this morning of snow.

声なくば鷺うしなわむ今朝の雪
Koe nakuba sagi ushinawan kesa no yuki

Will it be puckery?
    I don't know;
  the first-picked persimmon.

渋かろか知らねど柿の初ちぎり
Shibukaro ka shiranedo kaki no hatsuchigiri

Nothing moving
    in either mountain or field;
  this snowy morning.

野に山に動くものなし雪の朝
No ni yama ni ugoku mono nashi yuki no kesa

Looking up,
    it stares at the plum tree;
  the frog.

仰向いて梅をながめる蛙かな
Aomuite ume wo nagameru kawazu kana

Daybreak;
    a confusion of mosquitoes
  at my pillow.

曙や蚊のうろたゆる枕元
Akebono ya ka no urotayuru makura moto

Butterflies
on the little girl's path,
in front and behind.

蝶々や女子の道の後先や
Chocho ya onago no michi no atosaki ya

HASHIMOTO TAKAKO

(1899–1963)

Hashimoto Takako was born in the Hongo area of Tokyo her father a government official. A musical child, she began to study the koto at age six, and later, shamisen and piano. At age twelve, she dropped out of school because of pleurisy, but was well enough at eighteen to marry Hashimoto Toyojiro, an architect and businessman. Only a year later she was hospitalized with typhus. At twenty, she gave birth to the first of four daughters, the last of whom, Miyoko, would become a haiku poet.

Toyojiro built a house, named the Rozanso, in Kokura, Kyushu, which would become a sort of cultural salon. The poets Takahama Kyoshi and Sugita Hisajo were invited to an event there and the latter gave Takako her first instructions in haiku. In 1924, with Hisajo's guidance, she submitted her first verse to the literary magazine *Hototogisu*, one she had written on a trip to Hokkaido.

> The dandelions,
> so big;
> summer in Ezo[1]

In 1937, Toyojiro passed away and two years later the family gave up the Rozanso. They evacuated to Nara towards the end of the Second World War, where Takako became involved with the haiku community. In 1946, her friend and mentor, Hisajo, passed away, which added to Takako's physical deterioration that had begun with the death of her husband. Yet she was an

---

1. The old word for Hokkaido.

enthusiastic traveler. She had previously visited Shanghai, Hong Kong and Manila with her husband, and continued to take trips with her daughters along the Kiso Road.

Takako was hospitalized with stomach troubles in 1960, and in 1963 succumbed to liver and gall bladder cancer. In between hospitalizations she continued to travel, received various awards for her verses and appeared on national television.

❧   ❧   ❧

Takako's style was said to be feminine, plaintive and uneasy. The influence of both Kyoshi, who emphasized writing plain reality as it is, and that of the intensity of her close friend Sugita Hisajo can be detected in her verses:

> Entering the white peach,
>   the knife blade
> cuts through the seed.

> Pulling the futon
>   so my head can't be seen;
> I disappear altogether.

❧   ❧   ❧

Haiku by Takako

> Eating a butterfly;
>   should I permit them or kill them;
> mountain ants.

蝶食ひし山蟻を許すか殺すか
Chou kuishi yama ari wo yurusu ka korosu ka

Snow melting;
a dove's happy song
fills my breast.

雪解鳩よろこぶこゑを胸ごもらせ
Yukige hato yorokobu koe wo mune gomorase

A beetle flying away,
showing
its delicate behind.

甲虫飛んで弱尻見せにけり
Kabutomushi tonde yowajiri misenikeri

A snowy field;
Venus chasing
a crescent moon.

雪原に没る三日月を木星追ひ
Setsugen ni iru mikazuki wo mokusei oi

In a poolside chair,
not getting wet;
alone.

ノールサイドの椅子身をぬらさざる孤り
Puurusaido no isu mi wo nurasazaru hitori

Pulling the futon
so my head can't be seen,
I disappear altogether.

頭も見せず蒲団を被れば一切消ゆ
Atama mo misezu futon wo kabureba issai kiyu

Washing my hair
and enjoying
the lightning.

洗髪いなずまきては遊びけり
Senpatsu inazuma kite wa asobikeri

A spring moon;
here on earth,
cats are encountering cats.

春月や地上に猫が猫と会ふ
Harutsuki ya chijou ni neko ga neko to au

The green Kiso![2]
In the mountains, graves
all face the villages.

青木曽や山墓はみな村へ向く
Ao Kiso ya yama haka wa mina mura e muku

A mackerel sky;
I leave the house,
and quickly yearn for the house.

いわし雲家出てすぐに家を恋ふ
Iwashigumo ie wo dete sugu ni ie wo kou

---

2. The Kiso is the sixty-mile heart of the Nakasendo, the ancient road between Edo and Kyoto. It is also the name of the river that runs through it.

MITSUHASHI TAKAJO
(1899–1972)

MITSUHASHI TAKAJO WAS BORN in the town of Narita, on the eastern outskirts of Tokyo, home of the famous Naritasan Shinshoji temple, which was established in the year 940. Her father wrote *waka*, or classical Japanese poetry. At the age of eighteen, Takajo graduated from high school, moved to Tokyo and lodged with an elder brother, Keijiro. Keijiro also studied waka, and under his influence, Takajo too began to write poetry in this ancient form.

Takajo married Higashi Kenzo, a dentist who was also a haiku poet and he taught her how to write haiku. Over the years, the two of them joined various haiku communities. In 1936, Takajo joined the staff of the literary magazine *Kon* and was put in charge of selecting verses for the women's haiku column.

In 1940, Takajo published a collection of her haiku, *Himawari* [Sunflowers]. Two years later, her eldest brother died and she succeeded to the head of the Mitsuhashi family, whose financial fortunes suffered a decline in the aftermath of the Second World War. It was around this time that she took the pen name of Mitsuhashi Takajo.

Takajo died at the age of seventy-three and is buried at the Naritasan Shinshoji temple.

※　　※　　※

Takajo wrote in her own unrestricted colloquial language. She is considered to have been the advance guard for writing poetry that conveyed women's emotions and thought, and in this way she reflected one of her early influences, Akiko Yosano (1878–1942) a controversial poet who was also a feminist and social reformer.

Seeing a dream in spring,
my eyelids
become damp.

Climbing this tree,
I'll become a witch;
evening autumn leaves.

In her later years, Takajo lived a more private life and her poetry was more subtly profound. She had perhaps become a religious ascetic, perhaps influenced by the esoteric Buddhist temple connected to her both in birth and in death.

Getting old,
I become a camellia,
dancing away.

Haiku by Takajo

Losing weight in the summer;
all the things I abhor
become abhorrent.

夏痩せて嫌ひのものは嫌ひなり
Natsu yasete kirai mono wa kirai nari

The season's first storm;
has pleased
everyone.

初嵐して人の機嫌はとれませぬ
Hatsuarashi shite hito no kigen wa toremasenu

Hurriedly chirping,
hastening to their death:
cicadas on trees.

啼き急ぐは死に急ぐこと樹の蝉よ
Naki'isogu wa shini'isogu koto ki no semi yo

Autumn dewdrops;
in the dying of the day, too,
I tighten my sash.

白露や死んでゆく日も帯しめて
Shiratsuyu ya shinde yuku hi mo obi shimete

The camellia falls
into the current
of an ancient, ancient stream.

椿落つむかしむかしの川ながれ
Tsubaki otsu mukashi mukashi no kawa nagare

The drooping of a wisteria;
something of this world
of a lingering old woman.

藤垂れてこの世のものの老婆佇つ
Fuji tarete kono yo no mono no rouba tatsu

Withered trees,
    withered trees in the mountains;
  breaking them, the smell of bones.

枯木山枯木を折れば骨の匂ひ
Kareki yama kareki wo oreba hone no nioi

When the wild ducks
    fly high, I become
  a white-haired old woman.

鴨翔たばวれ白髪の媼とならむ
Kamo kaketaba ware shiragami no oona to naran

An old nightingale;
    when its tears well up,
  it sings.

老鶯や泪たまれば鳴きにけり
Rou-ou ya namida tamereba nakinikeri

A thousand insects chirping;
    one crazy one
  chirping.

千の虫啼く一匹の狂い啼き
Sen no mushi naku ippiki no kurui naki

NAKAMURA TEIJO
(1900–1988)

NAKAMURA TEIJO WAS BORN in Kumamoto City in Kyushu. She was the only daughter of Saito Heijiro, a landowner who held the office of village chief. She graduated from a women's high school at age eighteen, began to submit haiku to the literary magazine *Hototogisu* and writing fan letters to Sugita Hisajo. In 1920, Teijo married Nakamura Shigeki, an official in the Kumamoto City finance department and traveled with him as he was transferred to Tokyo, Yokohama, Sendai, Nagoya and other parts of the country. Later, they settled down in Tokyo. Her eldest daughter, Ogawa Tomiko, also became a well-known haiku poet.

In 1921, Sugita Hisajo visited Teijo at home and this began a long series of interchange between the two. In 1934, Teijo became a staff member of *Hototogisu* and published her first collection of haiku, *Shunsetsu* [Spring snow]. After the war, she launched and managed the haiku magazine, *Fuka*, and throughout the latter part of her life received a number of awards and commendation for her verses.

Teijo died in Tokyo Women's Hospital at the age of eighty-eight. Her grave is located in a Jodo Shinshu temple in Tokyo.

❧   ❧   ❧

Despite her close relationship with Hisajo, the style of Teijo's verses was quite different from that of her friend and mentor, and she wrote with a gentle adherence to life:

Dandelions;
　　the sun forever
in the sky.

For a child with a cold,
　　acorns and walnuts
in the drawer.

Playing guessing games with a coughing child;
　　she won't let me stop,
there's no end to it.

Her work was sometimes referred to as "kitchen haiku," which
was considered a derogatory term by some. Nevertheless, Teijo
felt that the place of the common woman was the home, that the
center of her work was the kitchen, and this is where she found
the inspiration for many of her poems.

❧　　❧　　❧

Haiku by Teijo

Peeling a hardboiled egg,
　　how bright;
cloudy weather in spring.

ゆで玉子むけばかがやく花曇
Yude tamago mukeba kagayaku hanakumori

Looking back
  between the months and days,
the river of spring.

かへりみる月日のなかの春の河
Kaerimiru tsukihi no naka no haru no kawa

Even the children
  feel the pathos in the evening
of a spring drizzle.

子等さへも夕ぐれあはれ春しぐれ
Kora sae mo yuugure aware haru shigure

Waking from a dream,
  in the spring dawn, everyone
is far away.

夢さめて春暁の人みな遠し
Yume samete shungyou no hito mina tooshi

At the beginning of dawn
    a single
  cicada.

暁のその始りの蝉一つ
Akatsuki no sono hajimari no semi hitotsu

Washed hair,
  now it's so cool!
Combing it in the dark.

洗ひ髪今ぞ涼しく闇に梳く
Araigami ima zo suzushiku yami ni suku

Suddenly escaping,
    the darkness left by the firefly
is disturbing.

つと逃げし蛍の闇のみだれかな
Tsuto nigeshi hotaru no yami no midare kana

Washing my hair;
    dried under the moon,
the nape of my neck.

洗髪月に乾きしうなじかな
Araigami tsuki ni hosekishi unaji kana

Together with the children,
    laughing voices;
autumn twilight.

子とありて笑へる声や秋の暮
Ko to arite waraeru koe ya aki no kure

To the right and the left,
    autumn winds blowing;
clouds flowing.

右左秋の風吹き雲流れ
Migi hidari aki no kaze fuki kumo nagare

Hearing her mother cough,
    she looks up;
the child.

咳をする母を見あげてゐる子かな
Seki wo suru haha wo miagete iru ko kana

HOSHINO TATSUKO

(1903–1984)

HOSHINO TATSUKO WAS BORN in Tokyo, the second daughter of the famous poet and critic, Takahama Kyoshi, who taught her the techniques of haiku from an early age. In 1910, the family moved to the seaside town of Kamakura, south of Tokyo and at the age of twenty-two she married Hoshino Yoshito, a sculptor. It was from this time, with Kyoshi's encouragement, that she became involved with the haiku magazine *Hototogisu*. In 1930, again with Kyoshi's encouragement, she established the first periodical by women, *Tamamo*, and in 1932 she became a staff member of *Hototogisu*.

Beginning in 1953, her husband Yoshito became a sort of cultural ambassador and was sent first to North America and Brazil and later to India and Europe, accompanied by his wife.

Kyoshi passed away in 1959 and Tatsuko inherited his position as the selector of haiku for the *Asahi Shimbun* newspaper.

After a long and successful career in the haiku community, Tatsuko passed away in 1984 from colorectal cancer. She is buried at the Jufukuji Rinzai Zen temple in Kamakura, next to Kyoshi.

Tatsuko had a bright and carefree sensitivity which was reflected in her verse:

> I go bounding
>   up the stairs, forgetting
> my age.

She followed her father's preference for depicting the world objectively, and remaining faithful to the beauties of nature.

A winter butterfly
captures my soul
and flies about.

Kyoshi said that he had written his haiku to describe "life" and was happily aware that his daughter's verses had given his own style a new energy.

❧   ❧   ❧

Haiku by Tatsuko

Our first telephone.
And sure enough,
my father's voice.

初電話ありぬ果して父の声
Hatsu denwa arinu hatashite chichi no koe

First dream of the year;
while talking about it,
I forgot what it was.

初夢と話しゐる間に忘れけり
Hatsu yume hanashiiru ma ni wasurekeri

The child on the rocking horse
bows politely
and falls off.

竹馬の子のおじぎしてころびけり
Chikuba no ko no ojigi shite korobikeri

Keeping my left hand
on the spring brazier,
I read.

左手を春の火桶にあづけ読む
Hidarite wo haru no hioke ni azuke yomu

I feel pleasure
even in resenting
the spring rain.

春雨をうらむ心もたのしくて
Harusame wo uramu kokoro mo tanoshikute

Regretting the passing of spring,
regretting the passing of life,
are the same.

春惜み命惜みて共にあり
Haru oshimi inochi oshimite tomo ni ari

Everybody looks
at my Japanese clothes;
the slight heat of Paris.

皆が見る私の和服パリ薄暑
Mina ga miru watashi no wafuku pari hakusho

A remaining scent
    of the mosquito smudge;
    morning cleanup.

蚊遣火の香の残りたる朝掃除
Kayaribi no ka no nokoritaru asa souji

Eating peaches,
    smoking cigarettes;
    traveling alone.

桃食うて煙草を吸うて一人旅
Momo kuute tabako wo suute hitori tabi

I go bounding
    up the stairs, forgetting
    my age.

とんとんと上る階段年忘れ
Ton ton to agaru kaidan toshi wasure

BIBLIOGRAPHY

Works in Japanese

Fukumoto Ichiro, ed. *Seigetsu kushu.* Tokyo: Iwanami shoten, 2012.

Fukumoto Ichiro, ed. *Onitsura kushu/hitorigoto.* Tokyo: Iwanami shoten, 2018.

Hashimoto Takako. *Hashimoto Takako zenkushu.* Tokyo: Kadokawa bunko, 2018.

Hoshika Soichi, ed. *Sogi hokkushu.* Tokyo: Iwanami shoten, 1985.

Hoshino Takashi, ed. *Kidai betsu kushu/koro.* Kamakura: Kamakura Kyoshi Tatsuko Kinenkan, 2015.

Ikeuchi Osamu, ed. *Ozaki Hosai kushu.* Tokyo: Iwanami shoten, 2015.

Ito Kciko. *Sugita Hisajo no hyakka.* Tokyo: Furansuto, 2019.

Kira Sueo, ed. *Haika kijin dan/zoku haika kijin dan.* Tokyo: Iwanami shoten, 2009.

Kojima Noriyuki & Arai Eizo, ed. *Kokinwakashu.* Tokyo: Iwanami shoten, 1998.

Komura Zenko, ed. *Masaoka Shiki kushu.* Tokyo: Furansuto, 2007.

Kurita Yasushi, ed. *Hekigodo haikushu.* Tokyo: Iwanami shoten, 2011.

Masaoka Shiki. *Masaoka Shiki.* Tokyo: Chikuma shobo, 1992.

Murakami Mamoru, ed. *Santoka kushu.* Tokyo: Chikuma bunko, 2002.

Murayama Sadao, ed. *Ryokan no haiku.* Niigata-shi: Kokoto shoten, 2017.

Nakamura Shunjo, ed. *Basho haikushu*. Tokyo: Iwanami shoten, 1994.

Okada Isao. *Sogi*. Tokyo: Yoshikawa Hirobumi kan, 1998.

Oyama Sumita. *Haijin Santoka no shogai*. Tokyo: Yayoi shobo, 1984.

Sanseito Henshusho. *Konsaisu jimei jiten*. Tokyo: Sanseito, 1976.

Seisensui. *Seisensui kushu*. Tokyo: Shinsho bunko, 1943.

Shimizu Shozo. *Hana no haijin Kaga no chiyojo*. Tokyo: Alphabeto Books, 2017.

Sutejo wo yomikai, ed. *Sutejo kushu*. Osaka: Iwazumi shoin, 2016.

Takahama Kyoshi, ed. *Kyoshi kushu*. Tokyo: Iwanami shoten, 1983.

Tsuru Hisashi & Moriyama Takashi, ed. *Man'yoshu*. Tokyo: Ofusha, 1944.

Works in English

Blyth, R. H. *A History of Haiku, Volumes 1 & 2*. Tokyo: The Hokuseido Press, 1963.

Blyth, R. H. *Haiku, Volumes 1–4*. Tokyo: The Hokuseido Press, 1949.

Nishida, Kitaro. *An Inquiry into the Good*. Trans. by Masao Abe & Christopher Ives. Chelsea, Mich.: Yale University Press, 1990.

The Kokusai Bunka Shinkokai, ed. *Introduction to Classic Japanese Literature*. Tokyo: Kokusai bunka shinkokai, 1948.

Photo credits

p.17 Sakarin Sawasdinaka; p.22 Luis Gago; p.29 FocusStocker; p.46 mujijoa79; p.58 Myntsri; p.65 Lee Yiu Tung; p.72 Anna Repina; p.87 Tamu 1500; p.93 Nick Fedirko; p.102 worldlandscape; p.110 TakaH; p.128 Josiah_S; p.135 Sann von Mai; p. 158 Sabaidee; p.166 Aleksandr Ozerov; p.173 AndreAnita; p.181 martinho Smart; p.184 hxdbzxy; p.189 Sakarin Sawasdinaka; p.193 Morningstar Sun; p.197 Scott Wilson Photography; p.203 Edy Pamungkas; p.220 G Allen Penton. p. 223 jserp. All Shutterstock.

"Books to Span the East and West"

Tuttle Publishing was founded in 1832 in the small New England town of Rutland, Vermont [USA]. Our core values remain as strong today as they were then—to publish best-in-class books which bring people together one page at a time. In 1948, we established a publishing office in Japan—and Tuttle is now a leader in publishing English-language books about the arts, languages and cultures of Asia. The world has become a much smaller place today and Asia's economic and cultural influence has grown. Yet the need for meaningful dialogue and information about this diverse region has never been greater. Over the past seven decades, Tuttle has published thousands of books on subjects ranging from martial arts and paper crafts to language learning and literature—and our talented authors, illustrators, designers and photographers have won many prestigious awards. We welcome you to explore the wealth of information available on Asia at www.tuttlepublishing.com.